Cup of Tea Tales
The Early Years

David M Cameron

ISBN: **9798712065288**

DEDICATION

For all the teachers who ever taught me and made primary school such a joy. In particular, Miss Blackmore and Mr Kelly from Stainbeck Preparatory School and Harehills County Primary School respectively, thank you!

CONTENTS

ACKNOWLEDGMENTS

For Olwyn, as always!

OPENING UP THE MEMORY AS FAR BACK AS IT WILL GO

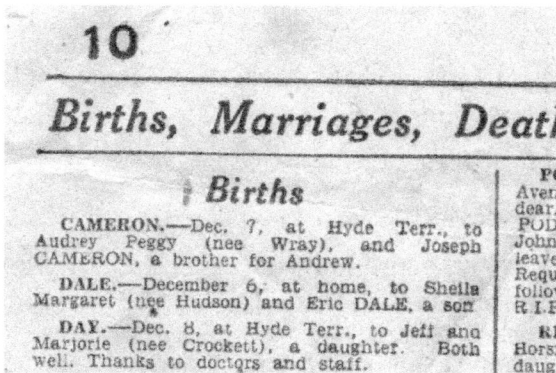

10

Births, Marriages, Deatl

Births

CAMERON.—Dec. 7, at Hyde Terr., to Audrey Peggy (nee Wray), and Joseph CAMERON, a brother for Andrew.

DALE.—December 6, at home, to Sheila Margaret (nee Hudson) and Eric DALE, a son

DAY.—Dec. 8, at Hyde Terr., to Jeff and Marjorie (nee Crockett), a daughter. Both well. Thanks to doctors and staff.

Last night I was considering what I might tell you about life in Leeds in the 1950s-60s. As I thought about these times, the memories came pouring out. It was like taking the top off a pop bottle that had been shaken, and it came frothing out uncontrollably. The interesting thing is that one memory leads to others that you had long forgotten. The tastes, the sounds, the smells come back and take you by the hand to those times of youth and innocence. Oh, how the world has changed! My father used to tell me that he wrote on slates at primary school in Scotland and I thought he must have lived in the Stone Age and here I am doing it too. My children will think just the same of me.

I was born in Hyde Terrace Maternity Hospital in December 1954 and I can't remember that, but I do remember my first house. We lived at 36 Lawrence Avenue, which was on the right as you reached the top of Easterly Road just before the roundabout at Oakwood Lane. The Street consisted of small semi-detached houses and ours was two bedroomed. It backed onto the large council housing estate

3

of Gipton. Our family at that time consisted of my parents, older brother and me.

I have memories of sitting with my mother when 'Listen With Mother' was on the radio. The stories and songs used to entertain me and my mother would have a few minutes of quiet time. Afterwards, I would sit playing with toy cars, soldiers or something similar. My mother told my wife that when I was little all I needed was a cardboard box and I was happy for hours. These were pre-school times and I started school at four years old.

At the top of Easterly Road near the junction with Arlington Road were shops on both sides of the road. I remember going with my mother to the greengrocer's and she would ask for two pounds of potatoes and the shopkeeper would scoop them out of a hessian sack, or sometimes out of a box arrangement which was open at the bottom, a little like a giant bird feeder, so when potatoes were removed from the bottom they were replaced from those stored above. The scoop was a silver bowl and the shopkeeper estimated the order, placed them on the scales, added weights and maybe added or removed a potato or two. He would then pour them directly into my mother's shopping bag. Carrots might be next and the same procedure took place and the vegetables were all loose in the bag. There were no fridges and so shopping was an everyday occurrence and, as we walked to the shops, you could only buy what you could carry.

Other shops that were there were two butchers', one on either side of the road. I remember they were Dewhurst's on the left side as you looked away from Harehills and Dyson's on the right. Dewhurst's was the bigger of the two. Both shops had large, very thick wooden chopping boards, and I was fascinated to see the butcher chop meat whilst we waited. Sometimes, they wore a chain mail gauntlet and they sliced and cut the meat with razor sharp knives. They had bacon slicers and I am not sure whether it was the chopping or slicing that caused Mr. Dyson to lose a finger, but he had certainly lost most of one. As a young lad, I used to listen with interest to the banter between the butchers and the women shopping. It was always good humoured and probably, looking back with adult eyes, a little cheeky.

There was also a fish and chip shop. The name came back to me last night and I believe it was called Youngman's. It was similar to the one at Oakwood in the fact that it was decorated in the Art Deco style. There were highly polished finishes and counters and leaded windows. I remember the one in Youngman's depicting the tale of the Pied Piper in bright colours. Looking back, it seemed an odd tale for a fish shop, but it also had brightly coloured tiles, windows and mirrors, most of which had fish or fish scenes. I recall that people would queue out of the door when it was open as it had a good reputation and was very popular. Who could resist haddock or cod and chips, with scraps? Our arteries must have loved it!

There was a Post Office and it was here that my mum would wait to collect her family allowance, have her book stamped and then be given the cash. I would often be allowed a Lucky Bag, if I was good, and I remember the excitement of opening it up to see what mysteries were inside, usually a couple of tattoo transfers, skull and crossbones, heart with a knife through it, a few sweets and a gob stopper. I can't remember there ever being much.

There was a grocer's and here biscuits were bought out of large biscuit boxes and again they were spooned into the silver weighing dish, weighed and then poured into large paper bags. The shopkeeper would skilfully hold the corners of the bags, swing the bags around to fasten them and then add them to the growing collection of shopping in the shopping bag. There was no plastic of any sort at these times. There was also a bakery and on special occasions mum would go in and buy me a gingerbread pig. I loved them. She would also buy a fresh cream cake and that would carefully be carried home to share out later.

Where we lived was probably an area for up-and-coming families. The houses were privately owned and my father was an engineer. He worked at Catton's Steel Foundary in Black Bull Street, Hunslet and he was the Chief Inspector of Steel Castings at one time. As a young man he was doing well at work and in his career. I remember that when we got our first car it was one of very few in the street and I believe that when we got our black and white television set, it was the first and neighbours would come around to have a look at it. The picture quality would be laughable now as it would flicker and you would need to adjust the vertical and horizontal hold on the cathode ray tube. Sometimes my father would fix problems with a swift smack to the side of the set, but my brother and I were never allowed to do so. What it did bring into mine and my brother Andrew's world were children's programmes. Who could forget Muffin the Mule, Rag, Tag and Bobtail, The Woodentops and the spottiest dog you ever saw, Andy Pandy, Sooty with Harry Corbett? What joys! Parents must have loved it! We would sit and watch Children's Hour and there would not be a sound from either of us.

TV was very different in those days. The voices of the presenters were so posh it was unbelievable. There were intermissions, test cards and sometimes services would be broken and you were informed they would be resumed soon. Variety shows were the main adult entertainment and there were quiz shows, such as Double Your Money. Fillers were the Westerns and Roy Rogers and Trigger, Champion the Wonder Horse and The Lone Ranger fulfilled our boyish dreams of excitement. Robin Hood with Richard Greene and William Tell gave another angle to the American influence. Who could resist booing at the Sheriff of Nottingham or Gessler?

In 1957, Pinky and Perky was one of the first puppet shows and it linked popular music with comedy. Other delights were: Torchy the Battery Boy in 1960 where Gerry Anderson was the producer, Four Feather Falls ran until 1960, again with Gerry Anderson, Supercar 1961-62, and later Thunderbirds. Simply animated cartoons such as Noggin the Nog 1959-65 and Captain Pugwash were performed with cardboard cut-outs in 1957. "Coddling catfish!" they were good.

Who can forget the joys and frustration of getting a stable picture, without ghosting on the TV?

LAWRENCE AVENUE, ADVENTURES.

While still living in Lawrence Avenue, my mother was pregnant with my younger brother and as this was her third, it was to be a home birth. In those days, home help was provided and Mrs. Killfeather was dispatched to the house. The woman terrified me and I am not sure if it was her ultra-efficient manner, not unlike a kind of Mary Poppins but without the warmth, or the fact that she was not my mum. I suppose she would only have been about for a few days, but she was much stricter than Mum and I can only remember one redeeming feature and that was that she made wonderful lemon cheese pies. She called them sun pies and the pastry was divine and the bright lemon curd had thin radials of pastry like the spokes of a wheel. The pies looked very much like the sun to me. Anyway, my elder brother and I couldn't wait for the birth so that she would be gone.

The day arrived and I remember watching William Tell on the television when the midwife came down to speak to us. It was just as the adverts came on midway through the programme and it was at a really exciting bit. With reluctance, we both trudged up the stairs to see mum holding our new younger brother, Stuart. At the time, I was eager to leave and get back to the programme, but alas that wasn't to be the case and I saw time slipping away as we stood around looking at a tired mother and a not very exciting younger brother. It has taken a long time to completely forgive him for his timing, but he did become much more exciting as he grew. I don't think I ever discovered the ending to the episode, but as it was back the next week, I assumed William Tell saved the day.

One good thing his birth did result in, was Mrs. Killfeather leaving and things getting back to almost the same as they had been. It was not the end of Mrs. Killfeather though. She made a return as the villain in my novel, Wickergate, where she is an evil headmistress. To Mrs. Killfeather and her relatives, I must give my apologies. I am sure that she was a truly lovely lady and that my feelings were those of an easily excited child with a fervent imagination.

Me in the infamous pram

Shortly after the birth, there was a bit of excitement that involved my new brother. Mum was getting ready to take us to the shops. Baby brother was in his pram, fixed in with a harness, and I had been put on the back, sitting by the handle bar. For those not of my age, prams were very different from the complex devices used nowadays. They were more like a small bath supported on four wheels and I suppose were based on the design of a horse drawn carriage. Silver Cross was the Rolls Royce of the pram world and I believe they were made near Guisley, not far from Harry Ramsden's Fish restaurant, but I don't think ours would have been that fancy. Anyway, I was left sitting there and mum went back into the house. I was only about three years old, with my legs dangling down. I wasn't very comfortable and just shuffled myself to get a better position when the pram overbalanced. The back shot downwards and my younger brother's end shot upwards and the whole thing turned over on top of me and my baby brother hit the pathway with his head. Mum rushed out, had a panic and then righted the pram. I was fine and she was almost hysterical with worry for said sibling. I believe that was the last time I ever got to ride pillion with my brother, and looking back, I can now understand why.

My brother was none the worse for his adventure, but in hindsight, some unkind folk could suggest that maybe that accident was just desserts for spoiling William Tell? What a thought! Actually, being the youngest would have had some disadvantages as he wanted to join me and my brother as we played, but he wasn't quite up to it for quite a few years.

Andrew and I did play a lot together despite our age difference, about four years. I wish I could say that it was uneventful, but he was a little accident prone. Whilst still at Lawrence Avenue, we had a hot spell and I remember him doing some simple gardening. He was using an adult garden fork and he was wearing wellington boots. Things had been going well and I think we had a little plot where we grew vegetables from seeds. The soil in Leeds was incredibly heavy boulder clay. If the ground was wet it stuck like thick glue, and if there was a dry spell the clumps would set hard like concrete. You can probably imagine what was going to happen, but unfortunately my brother couldn't. He was digging with gusto and pushed down hard with the fork. His mind had wandered and the fork went though rubber wellington, his foot, and back out through the sole of the boot. I don't remember a scream, more a slow realisation of what had happened. Instinctively, he must have withdrawn the fork and hobbled back inside to our long suffering mother. The boot was removed, the word 'stupid' was used a few times. There was a copious amount of blood, quick bandaging after cleaning of the wound, followed by a trip to Dr. Black's for a tetanus injection.

I would like to say that he and I learned from such experiences, but that was not the case. At this time, young children were allowed to play with things that parents would die of shock if they saw today. I remember something, possibly a shed, had been demolished and it was another hot spell and I was playing in the garden when I stood, barefoot, on a piece of wood lying on the ground that had a nail sticking through it. Following in the family tradition, the force drove the nail right into my foot and it hung there trailing the plank of wood. I am sure that I screamed and had to balance in pain as I didn't dare put my foot down as it would have driven the nail in further.

Mother must have been on some kind of tranquilisers, or maybe she was just a saint, dealing with our frequent accidents, but she rushed out, held my leg, sat me down and against my wishes, just pulled the wood and nail out of my foot. This adventure was followed by the regular visit for the tetanus shot after bathing, cleaning and dressing the wound.

My big brother did excel himself on one further incident that involved his best friend from further up the street. We were all in the garden playing and there was a wooden garage. The garage was full of my father's tools and old tins of paint, bags of cement and a collection of items, that I didn't recognise. I am sure that in our comics there was a character called Mick Mercury and he was an idol. He could do dangerous things and live to tell the tale. Anyway, we were in swimming costumes and I think we had a tin bath full of water. It must have been another hot day. Number one brother was reliving an adventure and he decided to torture his friend in the garage. No pain was involved, I might add, but red mastic powder was. Andrew, for some reason beyond me, decided to rub his friend's hair with the red powder and it came up a treat. His friend had bright red, stiff hair and scalp, but unfortunately it did not come out as easily as it went in. Mum must have looked in on us to see how we were doing, whilst she was busy with younger baby brother. She almost had a fit. This time she did panic! Our friend's hair was shampooed, rinsed and repeated over and over, but still his blond locks maintained their now orange-red colour. I don't know how long this went on for, but she would still be doing it now, if she hadn't been frightened his hair would all fall out.

Eventually, she had to own up. She led the boy back to his home and suffered a very irate mother, who said she would never allow her son to play with us again. This wasn't an idle threat, as she never did. I do know that his hair eventually returned to his natural colour, but if like me he later lost most of it, I wonder who he and his mother would have blamed?

I don't think we were an unusual family. I just think that no one tells you the joys of raising children, and three boys certainly must have taken my mother to the limit and beyond on many occasions. Things were very different and my childhood was a magical time, full of adventures mishaps and experiences I wouldn't have missed for the world.

MY GRANDMOTHER'S HOUSE

I have many memories of my childhood, as I suppose most other people do of their own. In my case, the memories are all good and it truly was a magical world for me. In my mind, many of my childhood experiences are in black and white, which is probably linked to television that was in its infancy and was in monochrome, and also due to the pollution that had created buildings that were indeed black. In Leeds and northern cities, the stonework in town halls, museums, factories, schools, and statues was black due to the smoke from thousands of coal fires and factory chimneys.

Regent Terrace

One splash of colour though, was my grandmother's house. Not the house itself, as that was a mix of stone and painted brick, but my grandmother herself and her kitchen. My grandmother was very short, very plump and she dyed her thinning hair a fairly vivid orange. Her dresses were shapeless and often of floral design, but quite colourful. Her skin was bright pink and she had hands that were amazing, in hindsight. She had the ability to plunge them into almost boiling water to wash up and showed no sign of discomfort.

I loved my grandmother and her hugs were smothering and comforting in the way that all grandparents' hugs should be, and she was always kind to me. Anyway, I should tell you about the house. It still stands all these years later and hopefully will continue long after I have left the Earth. It was a two-up two-down terrace in Chapel Allerton in Leeds, in the North of England. There were about nine houses in the row and the road was unmade. For some reason it is a private road and despite there being some large, grand houses in the street, it was unsurfaced: no cobbles, no bitumen, just dirt, until quite recently. It sits opposite a beautifully kept park, bowling green and a large number of allotments. In the past, the hillside of the park had air raid shelters, but these were filled in many years ago. There was a bit of waste land at the end of the terrace, opposite the bowling green, with some large trees set on a small hillock and I vividly remember a tiny bakery built into the hillside. It was like some sort of hobbit building but unfortunately it is no longer there. I remember with great pleasure going with grandma to buy tiny freshly baked loaves. They were individual size and when cut in two, spread with jam and butter and eaten whilst still warm, were delicious. Another delight was the bilberry and cream individual pies. They were grandma's favourite and I can still taste them as I think about them. I had forgotten all about them until I was writing this. The little bakery was dug into the hillock and there was a rough stone wall holding the hill in place. A chimney vented fumes from the oven and there was only a small counter, but a strong smell of bread and baking.

Another vivid, but not so pleasant memory was of the slugs that would appear on the bakery wall. If there is a world record for slug size, then Chapel Allerton must have it. They were monsters, at least seven inches of black, slimy creatures, the subject of nightmares. They also inhabited the stone wall opposite the back entrance to grandma's house and her garden. My grandma was not overly sentimental and she dealt with the slugs without mercy. Salt was her chemical weapon of choice. After a liberal dousing by my grandma, I watched in fascinated horror as the creatures writhed in a slow agony, frothing and foaming as the salt dehydrated them and ensured they never trespassed into her domain again. Ever since, I have never resorted to using this approach to dealing with the pest as it was remarkably cruel.

The little house was a marvel to me. Outside on the dirt road was a gas street lamp, just like the one in The Lion, The Witch and the Wardrobe and the toilets were not in the house, but in a row at the bottom of the lane. The houses didn't have toilets at that time and my brothers and I were amused by the Guzunders. These were large chamber pots, ready for those times when a walk down the lane was either too much of an effort, or the thought of the weather, the cold and the dark, proved too much of a barrier. Each house had its own loo and there was a large iron key on a piece of string for when nature called. The toilets are not there now, another conquest of modernity and the passing of hygiene and sanitation laws that we have benefitted from.

Anyway, I'll have to leave you hanging there, a bit like the key on the string, but I'll be back soon. I always liked visiting my grandma's.

LAUNDRY, BATHING AND COAL DELIVERY

As I said, I loved my grandma and her house, but I didn't mention my grandfather, Harry. Harry had been a tailor, but he had also owned his own sweet and tobacconist's shop after the war and run the snooker hall in Chapel Allerton. His favourite pub was the Nag's Head and he was a regular for many years. My grandfather, like my grandmother, was short and had a bit of a pot belly and his kingdom was the front room. The house consisted of a kitchen and a lounge, two bedrooms and a cellar. There was neither bathroom nor toilet when they first lived there and the bath was a galvanized metal tub that hung on a hook on the wall of the steps leading down into the cellar.

Here where I now live in Western Australia, the English have a reputation for being shy of soap and not bathing regularly. In Perth a minimum of two showers a day and more in the very hot summer weather is the norm, but in the

cold English climate, it takes courage to shed one's clothes. Certainly, in the days before a bathroom was fitted, bathtime was a once a week affair. There were only two sources of hot water in the house and initially only one. The kitchen was dominated by a large black cast-iron range. For the uninitiated, a range was a fireplace cum oven and it had hot plates on either side. Kettles and pans could be heated from the coal fire that burned at its centre; meals could be cooked and it was the equivalent of a working class Aga.

On bath night, the bath would be brought out and placed in the centre of the kitchen. Water was heated and the bath filled. My grandfather would have been first, as men were dominant. He would soap himself with a bar of carbolic soap and then rinse himself with a jug of hot water. I believe grandma would have been next, using the same water, as it was too time-consuming and costly to heat fresh. In younger families the children would have followed on in chronological order, all using the same water. Oh, the joys of being the youngest in a large family!

I never experienced the tin bath, as grandma had another delight up her sleeve for us and that was the kitchen sink. I can't quite remember if it was a stone sink or just a heavy duty porcelain one, but if we needed a bath, and grandma was the decider on that, we were stood in the sink, naked to the world, and I mean the world, as the sink was adjacent to a window and we were scrubbed mercilessly. As the saying went, 'cleanliness is next to godliness' and so we must have been very pure. We were rubbed until we were bright pink and the drying process was no better. The towel would be coarse and rough and this added to the lack of skin on the finished article. Grandma seemed to want to particularly dry us 'round the houses', which was her euphemism for the more delicate nether regions. Delicacy was not in my grandmother's vocabulary, but the term "round the houses' has stuck and I used it for one of my music album titles.

I am sure that a number of the passing residents, Mrs Orange or Miss Clarkson, would have looked in, and given their seal of approval over the thoroughness of my grandmother's technique. I suppose it was a bit like having a well-scrubbed doorstep, a well-scrubbed grandchild was another mark of social standing.

The front room, or parlour, was a dark and rather damp room, probably because the fire wasn't always lit, whereas the one in the kitchen was. Originally, I remember the fittings for gas lights on the wall, but I don't think I was born when they were used. The house had electric lights, when I look back. There was a piano for a time, but I don't know if anyone ever played it. It was an upright and had still got candle holders on each side of the front. The room had a number of things that captured my young imagination. Firstly, the fireplace housed an open fire and the lighting technique involved wood kindling, rolled up newspaper and then large chunks of coal. It was not smokeless at this time and they were primitive chunks of shiny black fossilised wood. To enhance the lighting process, a large sheet of newspaper was placed across the front of the fireplace to cause an updraft of air through the bottom, making the fire roar with the additional oxygen. The flames illuminated the sheet of paper and if not carefully managed, it would burst into flames. The fire was magic and had a strong smell of wood, smoke and dustiness. I would sit entranced as the coal burned, little geysers of coal-gas would burst out of the coal and in my imagination it was hell fire, another planet or the inside of a volcano. I remember watching it for hours. The greatest thrill was being able to break the coal and stir it using the metal poker. It was only when I was older that I was allowed, but I used to watch my brother do it. Even the cleaning out of the fire, when it was cold, was magical. The ash was white and so fine. There was a little brass set of brush and pan, just for the job and a matching poker. The tiled section in front of the fire had to be carefully swept and the dust and coke placed into the metal dustbin outside.

Sometimes when I was in the house, the coalmen would arrive. The truck barely managed to reverse part way down the narrow lane and dirty men with leather aprons and jackets would carry sacks of very heavy coal and tip them down a chute that allowed the coal to slide into the cellar. My brother and I would have to go down into the whitewashed cellar and move the coal heap into a separate section where the coal was stored. It always seemed a mystery and still does, why cellars were whitewashed, but they all were, or so I believe. Particularly large chunks of coal had to be broken up with a sledge hammer and then together we would carry a metal bucket, struggling with the weight, back up into the kitchen.

The cellar was only small and during the war doubled up as an air-raid shelter, I was told. The air was cold and it was always damp. At the top of the steps down was the tin bath, but facing you as you turned a corner was a meat safe. A meat safe was an equivalent of a fridge. It was a pink metal box with small holes for ventilation. The safe was where meat, milk, butter and other perishables were kept for short times. I believe it was made of metal to prevent rats or mice gaining access.

Down in the cellar was also where the washing took place. I can still recall a corrugated galvanized tub like a large barrel and there was a wooden thing called a dolly. It was like a small three-legged stool with a pole from the centre of where the seat would have been, with a crossbar at the top. Originally, washing would be put in the filled tub, soap added and then the dolly would be placed into it and rotated from side to side. This acted as a washing machine agitator, but was all physical exercise and woman-powered. Wet washing was pulled out, rinsed and then run through the mangle. The mangle was two rollers which turned with a heavy handle. The iron contraption was very effective. The clothes were fed in between the rollers and as they turned they squeezed the water out of the washing. The water ran back into a bucket and, in more modern versions, it was housed over the tub and the water just flowed back in. I loved to see sheets and shirts go in. The air could get trapped and the sleeve might blow up like a balloon before the air and water were forced out and the flat, stiff washing appeared out the other end. Over the years I visited my grandmother, new technology came into the house. The dolly was replaced by an electric tub with an agitator that worked by electricity. Mangles became electric and finally were replaced by the twin tub, with separate sections, one for washing and the other housing a spin dryer. My grandmother must have been delighted and blessed electricity.

Another use for the range was for heating irons. Irons in those days were exactly that. Small, but heavy, they were a similar shape to the electric iron, but there were solid iron and had to be heated. As a result, they worked in tandem, one being heated on the range whilst the other was being used. It took great skill not to burn the clothes, but I suspect there were failures over the years. One major difference in the clothes my grandfather wore was the shirts. Shirts had detachable collars that buttoned on and off. This allowed a well-dressed man to wear a clean collar every day. The shirt remained the same all week, but a clean collar was essential. The other fashion difference for the working man was that a suit might be worn, but for some reason the trousers came up to almost the armpit and a belt or braces would hold them in place. Shoes were always well polished and no self-respecting man like my grandfather would be seen out with dirty shoes.

Whilst I am writing this, so many memories that I had forgotten have come flooding back and added to the joy of the times I had with both my maternal grandparents. They were a funny couple, but I adored them and they always spoilt me and my brothers.

PIPES, GRASS CUTTING AND FIREWORKS

Harry Wray - Grandad with pipe.

My grandma's first name was Mary, but I never called her that. Mary and Harry Wray. Children would never have dreamt of calling adults by their first names in those days and I never called my parents by their first names. Harry would sit in the parlour, when we were there, probably to be out of the way, and it allowed him to read the newspaper and smoke his pipe. Pipe smoking fascinated me. I loved the smell of his pipe tobacco and pipe smoking was a ritual that I watched with fascination. Pipes had to be dismantled and pipe cleaners used to remove the tar residue and there was a tool that was used to bore out the bowl of the pipe and to keep it clean. The bowl, on one of his pipes, also screwed off the stem and here there was a reservoir of tar in the metal bowl that needed to be cleaned. My grandfather had a rack with a wide assortment of pipes and there seemed to be an art in cleaning, packing, lighting and keeping the tobacco burning. I can still smell it and see him sitting in his chair, contentedly puffing on his pipe. Of course, these were the days when the dangers of smoking were not so well known.

Grandma was the one who looked after me and my two brothers. We were not always there en masse, but one of the highlights was her cooking. Now, looking back, I am not sure if it was because she doubted my mother's culinary skills, or whether she just loved seeing us eat, but her cooking would have been close to being able to feed the 'five thousand'. Let me run you through the usual menu. We would start off with a tin of Heinz tomato soup, followed by traditional Yorkshire pudding. The pudding was cooked in a large tray maybe fourteen inches by ten. I think she may have cooked two trays if the three of us were there. The pudding would be cut in half, so it was a large portion. I had gravy on mine, but my elder brother had Golden Syrup on his. I have never tasted Yorkshire pudding that came close to hers. It was thin, light and crispy.

These two courses were starters and then we had a roast beef, roast potato and vegetable dinner. Again, she was not mean with her portions and to follow all this we had either the fabled bilberry and cream pie or more often Ambrosia tinned creamed rice pudding. My elder brother Andrew used to have a dollop of jam in the middle, but I never liked that. Afterwards we used to just have to lie around pogged for a while. You would imagine after a regular feed like this that we would have been quite large, but not one of us has ever had a real problem with weight. I can still taste and feel the effects as I write this now.

There was one memorable occasion where my elder brother, my grandma and I went to the local shops at Chapel Allerton and she bought a paper bag of Victoria plums. These were quite a thrill as they were quite expensive and only had a short season. We went back to the park and sat on a bench by the bowling green. It was the morning on a warm summer day and the bowling green was deserted. The grass was a lush dark green and the crown was immaculately kept. My grandmother handed out the plums and we tucked in. The plums were juicy and I was well into mine when grandma suddenly stopped and with her expert eye examined the plum she had. She snatched my brother's off him and checked that and then took mine. I looked before I handed it over and there were white maggoty things inside and, what was worse, I had clearly eaten some. She laughed, put the remains back in the bag and I believe we headed off to the ice cream van as compensation. I suspect she never told my mother what had happened, but I was always careful to check in future.

Grandma was fairly ingenious in occupying three small, active boys and she would often set us the task of cutting her grass. Now, as mentioned in a previous account, the lawn was tiny, probably about four square metres, five square yards. She did have a small hand powered lawn mower, but only my elder brother was allowed to use that and often it was almost impossible to use. She had a hierarchy of cutting utensils: a pair of shears for the eldest Andrew, large scissors for me and tiny scissors for my younger brother, Stuart. After struggling cutting for a while, blisters would appear on my fingers and the process became far from pleasant. The three of us toiled away until the job was done and then we would reap some reward. At least we gave her some peace and quiet for a little while.

One of the highlights of the year was Bonfire Night. November the fifth used to be a major event at the time and every year we would be taken by my grandma to the post office on Harrogate Road to buy a box of Standard Fireworks, a packet of sparklers and a rocket. Anyone could buy fireworks in those days and health and safety hadn't really been invented. They were fantastic. They smelt of gunpowder and magic and we all had a box. We used to take them home, carrying them as if they might explode at any time, which was probably the case.

The night would approach and when we were young, the letting off of the fireworks took place at home in the back garden. A small fire was built and lit, potatoes were placed in it to cook and we would stand around, burning hot on one side and freezing cold on the other. My father would set up milk bottles for the rockets, nail the Catherine Wheels to the fence and generally take charge. It was usually bitterly cold and frosty, and we gathered around as my dad lit the blue touch paper as instructed and stood well back. There was a moment when you felt it hadn't worked, followed by a whoosh or a roar. There was the excitement of the Roman Candles, the Spitfire, the Jack in the Box that always seemed to follow you around and, my favourite, Mt. Vesuvius.

We were allowed to hold the sparklers and we drew pictures in the night sky and they had a distinctive smell. Usually the whole evening was over in a very short time and we would stay watching the fire burn down, before pulling out the potatoes and eating dirty jacket potatoes with melted butter. What joy! Sometimes we had gingerbread pigs or gingerbread men.

Of course there would be the odd falling out, but my grandmother never seemed to lose her temper with us. She taught us to play cards and I can still remember hours of playing Pump the Well Dry and Snap and I know I used to get upset if I thought she was letting my younger brother win. The competitive streak has always been part of sibling rivalry, but I loved the time we all spent together.

CHRISTMAS AT MY GRANDMA'S

Christmas was always a magical time, especially as the family used to come together for Christmas parties. On Christmas Day, the party was at our house and my uncle, aunty, cousin and grandparents, Harry and Mary, all came around, but on Boxing Day we went to my Grandma's. As I have mentioned before, the house was hardly spacious, but we all fitted in and it was a merry old time. Uncle Ernest, Dad and Grandad would soon head off to the Nag's Head, whilst the ladies would busy themselves making sandwiches etc. What sticks in my mind the most were the games we would all play. Simple, but at the time, the only occasion we ever played them. One involved dropping 'dolly pegs', split wooden clothes pegs, into glass pint milk bottles. Each competitor, which was everyone, would stand, hold the peg at waist height and try and drop it into the bottle. We had about three or four turns each and the one with the most at the end of the round was the winner. Of course, most bounced off the edge to rounds of laughter and the occasional one went in. The children did have a distinct advantage being nearer to the bottle and often one of us would be the winner. I don't remember prizes, but maybe we did have them.

Another game was 'The Ring that is Passing'. A ring, often one of the wedding rings, was threaded through a long piece of string and the string tied off. One person stood within the ring of string and all the other players held the string with both hands and chanted, 'The ring that is passing has just passed by,' and all the hands were moved from left to right, disguising where the ring was and sometimes passing it from one to the other. The person in the middle had to touch the hand of the person that they thought had it. That person opened their hand and if the ring was there they swapped over. If not, then the game continued. It was great fun for us and after a few drinks, great fun for the adults. Simple times, but they had a magic that may have been lost, or maybe I've just grown elder.

Other games could be played such as 'Pass the Parcel' and even the ubiquitous 'The Parson's Cat'. In the Parson's cat you took turns to say, 'The Parson's Cat was a ....' and you inserted a word starting with 'A'. You had to be quick and you were out if you hesitated or couldn't think of or repeated a word. Once it had been around the room with 'A' it then continued and this time with 'B' etc. If someone was out the next person started again and this time with the next letter. Some letters were very easy, but some proved very challenging. Fun, silly and also good for extending children's vocabulary.

Sometimes we were expected to perform and as we got older violins might have to be played and our cousin, the only daughter of Aunty Joan and Uncle Ernest, would play a short piece. My brother Andrew did too, on occasions, and it was the least pleasurable part of the evenings. As we got older, Spanish guitars would make an appearance and we even sang a carol or two.

One drawback was that the children had to pay a visit to the neighbours, Miss Clarkson and Mrs. Orange. I am not sure why I wasn't too keen, but it was a bit of a chore. Probably, it was just that I wasn't sure what to say. They were very kindly ladies, ancient and so old fashioned, even then. They would often give us a bar of chocolate or something and wish us Happy Christmas. Really my Grandma probably felt they needed some company at Christmas and the elderly like to see children. Anyway, the visits were only short and I hope the two ladies enjoyed them.

Prior to the arrival at my Grandma's on Boxing Day, we visited Aunty Maud and Aunty Ethel. I am not sure exactly what relations they were. I think they were cousins of my mother and her sister. Again they lived on their own and they were kindly, welcoming and always gave us presents. The visit gave my parents time to catch up with them and they seemed very posh. They lived in Chapel Allerton, in a cul de sac that backed on to the allotments and the park. The houses looked across Gledhow Valley and were large semi-detached houses with big gardens. We arrived before we had any time to become dishevelled, hair watered and combed down, shirts tucked in, shoes cleaned and manners similarly polished.

The houses had thick plush carpets of a very light colour and were definitely not child-proofed. We had to sit still, politely saying thank you and listening to adults talk about things we did not know or understand. One of their daughters, Dorothy, was sometimes there and she spoke with a particularly posh voice and she had almost white make up and red lipstick and cheeks. I was intimidated and the end of my world would have been to spill something on her carpet.

Aunty Maud was much older and a warm friendly lady. Many years later, my father and I would go around to cut her lawns when it became too much for her. My father once caught her in her eighties on the stairs, with one knee on the windowsill whilst she cleaned the window, with a drop down the stairs that would have killed her. She was a very determined lady and my dad was very fond of her.

At the end of the Christmas parties, tired boys would be herded into the back of the car, no seatbelts in those days, and we would often sleep all the way home.

CHAPEL ALLERTON ROOTS.

Grandma as a child (Right front)

As I have spoken about in the past, my grandma and grandad lived in Regent Terrace and I used to hear them talk about snooker. My grandad, Harry Wray was a keen and, I was led to believe, a fine snooker player in his day. I had also heard from conversations between my mother and grandma that they had lived at a snooker hall in Chapel Allerton. I remember that the building was still standing until at least when I was about fifteen (1968/9) as my brother Andrew and his wife were given the opportunity to become the caretaker and live on site. We went to have a look around at the time and because they were newly married and had a baby, they decided it was not for them. The floors were still just bare flag stones and there didn't appear to be many mod cons. The walls were damp and the wiring was ancient. It is a shame as the building was full of history, but it wasn't a home for a young couple. My grandma was disappointed as she would have loved another generation of the family to have lived there, even if they were Camerons and not Wrays. The really sad thing is that the building should have been preserved and would have added even more to the wonderful historic Chapel Allerton.

My mother passed away several years ago and it was within some

British Workman's Institute Chapel Allerton

of the photographs she gave me that I came across my only picture of my great grandmother and the home where my mother and aunt were born. My mother wrote on the back *'My Grandma at the British Workman's Institute, where Joan and I were born."* I have restored the photograph a little, and as there is only one lady shown I suppose that she is my great grandma, but it could be the little girl. The snooker cues that the men are holding confirm it was indeed a snooker hall. The building no longer exists, but my elder brother tells me that my grandad's name was on the honour board in the hall when we went to look around.

I only remember him as an old gentleman and he used to love going for a pint at The Nag's Head. I am not aware of who the little girl is in the picture or whether my great grandfather is also shown and I suppose I never will. I have looked at the photograph greatly enlarged and above the door is a sign that clearly says Prosperity Lodge. As far as I can work out it would have been taken in the late 1800s.

I know that my grandparents moved from the institute and during the Second World War they owned a sweet shop. I believe that my mum and aunt went to Bleheim Primary School in Leeds so it would have been nearby. Apparently, they weren't great business people and allowed customers to buy items on 'tick'. My mother told me they would just avoid the shop and my grandparents when they couldn't pay it back. My grandparents returned to Chapel Allerton later and bought a small terrace house, 6 Regent Terrace, where they remained for the rest of their lives. My grandad worked as a tailor in one of the factories that made 'ready to wear' suits, that Leeds became famous for.

Harry Wray as a young man, (Right) Love the shoes!

My grandad was always a pipe smoker and I loved to watch him clean and prepare his pipe. It was quite a ritual and I loved the smell of his pipe tobacco. He would sit in the parlour of the two up- two down terrace house, before the coal fire, read his newspaper and puff on his pipe. Grandma was always busy in the kitchen and she seemed to wait on him hand and foot. Later in the day, he would get his coat and hat and then head off to the Nag's Head and after a couple of pints return for his dinner. He was a gentle man, shy to the point of hiding from anyone who came to the door. He would very occasionally tell of being in the First World War with his brothers when a shell exploded next to them and his brother was buried under rubble, but they managed to free him just in time. I can still hear him sitting in his chair calling, "Mary! Mary! Cup of tea, Mary." and within a short space of time grandma would appear with a cup of tea and maybe a biscuit.

Mary Wray

The picture above shows my grandma, Mary, as a young woman. She was always a kind and generous lady who loved a laugh, loved a game of cards and later in life loved to go on day trips and holidays. The picture below shows Harry and Mary Wray on a holiday. I had no idea where it was until I checked the street sign. It says 'Winkle Street' and through the wonders of the internet I tracked Winkle Street to the Isle of Wight and there I found a photograph of the same building. It is the gatehouse at Westover Park and they must have been on an organised tour and I have no idea who the lady is with them, but it is likely half of a couple they met on the trip and I assume the husband would be the person taking the photograph.

This little journey through my photographs has reminded me how linked to Chapel Allerton my family is. My father's side was very different and I will delve into their history another time.

KEEPING THE GRANDCHILDREN BUSY.

Grandad, Aunty Joan (Right) and Mum

I am not sure exactly when it happened, but probably very early in the 1960s, the government removed the external row of toilets at the end of Regent Terrace and converted one bedroom in each house into a bathroom. This meant that my grandma's house had one large bathroom and one bedroom. It was a real improvement and saw the end of the 'Guzunders' and trips down the lane to the outside toilet. I never liked going with the key to visit their specific toilet as it was cold, damp and dark as they had no lights. This was a major step into the modern world and was part of the development of the welfare state and improving the lot of the poor. My generation has reaped the benefit of this societal change. I remember the range being removed and a modern tiled fireplace was installed as the water was heated through an immersion heater and the parlour became a much more pleasant room. The need to bring out the tin bath, or for us the ignominy of a bath in the sink, was now behind us, which was good as we were getting older.

Another change that had major implications, and was a good first step, was the introduction of 'smokeless coal'. I still feel this was a definite misnomer, but the new coal produced far less smoke and started the movement to cleaner air. The buildings of Leeds changed during this period as the sandblasting of the black stone edifices revealed the gleaming yellowy white structures that had been hidden and we saw the change from the monochrome city to one of colour. There was discussion, at the time, about whether the architects had intended them to be seen black and the first conversations about acid rain that had worn the edges of the sculptures and designs. This was a time of optimism, care of our fellow man and a belief that life could get better through advances in science and technology. It was a brave new world, which now seems to be becoming Orwell's '1984'

Anyway, as a child at my grandmother's, my elder brother and I were set to work on assisting Grandma and Grandad by painting the cellar. I think I have mentioned before that the house had a coal-chute under an iron cover on the pavement, underneath where the kitchen sink was. On coal delivery days a truck would reverse into the entrance of the lane and big strapping men, with leather aprons would back up to the truck and grab hold of a big hessian sack, that someone positioned on the edge of the platform. With a grunt, he would lift it onto his back and march down the street with a hundredweight of hard coal. The covers had been removed and they would tip the open sack down into the chute. There was a great crunching noise and the coal landed down into the cellar. I loved watching the delivery and they would ensure everyone got the right amount before they left. The men were covered in black coal dust and their white eyes stood out, as they chattered and joked and made light of their work. I wonder now how their bodies put up with the treatment. Dust on the lungs must have caused a lot of bronchial problems and as they got older they wouldn't have been able to carry such weight. I know how well they earned their Christmas Boxes, when they came for the last delivery before Christmas Eve. The Boxes were a tip for workers at Christmas and the origin to the naming of Boxing Day, when servants and trades people were given gifts, usually of money. Milkmen, postmen, binmen and coalmen all would come around for their Christmas Box. All just about gone now, the postmen are fighting for their relevance and the bin collection is mainly automated, or at least it is here in Western Australia.

The painting of the cellar was a job that never made a lot of sense to me. The coal and coal dust tended to form a black film over all it came into contact with. The coal was in its own section of the cellar, but there was a large opening with no door. The floor was stone flags and the air was cool all year round and had an earthy damp smell, that I have only ever experienced in cellars. Caves don't have the same aroma, even though they are often damper. Thinking about it, it was probably that there was no flow of air.

Cellar walls had to be white! I seem to remember that they were painted with something called distemper. (I have just checked this and distemper is a water based paint that allows water to pass through it, so it can be used on damp surfaces.) It was thin paint that needed a good stirring and we would paint the walls with a wide brush. It didn't seem to cover well, but it certainly brightened up the older white paint. I can only think the white would produce a lighter effect when the electric light was on and brighten up the cellar. Washing was still done down there and food was stored in the cool temperatures as there were no fridges at first. There was no damp course in the cellar and the flags allowed damp to rise.

We spent a long time painting and my brother and I toiled away, with the best enthusiasm we could manage. I remember almost collapsing by the time we had finished, with sore arms. We were given a quick scrub and luckily the distemper paint washed off. After my grandma's scrubbing, our arms were bright pink, well scoured and would cause no embarrassment if seen by the neighbours. Grandma was quick to revitalise us with some of her cooking and a few coins as payment. I am trying to think what she gave us to drink and I can't remember. It could have been orange cordial as it was around, in fact you could buy orange drinks from the milkman. It was the usual dinner: tomato soup, followed by Yorkshire pudding, followed by meat, potatoes and vegetables. We always had a pudding and often Ambrosia rice pudding out of a tin. My favourite dessert was chocolate steamed pudding , but often we had treacle pudding. These were Heinz puddings in a tin. You can still get them, I believe. You had to pierce the tin and then heat them in boiling water for a while. With custard, they were magnificent and something to die for, and such a diet probably contributed to many an early death, but what a way to go!

One thing I really loved was when she had fresh peas in their pods and we had to pop the pods to get to the peas. Some were so tasty and sweet, that I couldn't resist eating them. If I did it too much there would be a mild scolding, but I knew she never minded.

By the time we had finished lunch we would be too full to move. We would sit around and often play cards. A folding baize card table would sometimes come out, or we would sit in the front room at the small folding table. She knew a number of games and taught us, 'Pump the Well Dry', Pairs, Snap and Patience. We would play for hours and she seemed to enjoy it as much as we did. The only thing that annoyed me was when my younger brother started to play with us and my grandma would always ensure that he won. I always thought that was very unfair, but I am sure she did the same with me when playing with my elder brother. Grandad would sometimes play, but he became ill whilst I was still little. When we were older again, she taught us Whist and I really enjoyed it. When I was little I always enjoyed cards. The feel and look of the cards was special, almost magical. Leeds was the home of playing cards with Waddington's printing them from 1922.

Another interesting thing was her rugging and embroidery. She had what she called a 'peg rug' and it was a doormat made up of lots of small pieces of cloth. I know they were quite prized and were very robust. As I was getting older, I believe she got 'Readycut Rugs'. These were a kit where you bought a base with a printed pattern on it. It came with bundles of wool of various colours. Each piece was about two to three inches long. You made a loop and hooked into onto a tool, pushed it through the base at the right colour spot, looped it through and pulled it tight. It was a slow process, but eventually you produced a thick rug that was serviceable and had a design on it. My mother also became interested in these and made quite a few. We even had them bought as a Christmas present one year and my elder brother and I enjoyed doing them.

My grandma also loved embroidery and she, and many other elderly ladies, spent hours and hours producing wonderful tablecloths with exquisite designs and colours. I loved watching her work at it. She seemed very skilled and worked at quite a pace. My mother did a little, but her real love was knitting. Many were the hours she would sit with the clicking of needles, the pulling of wool, the staring at the pattern and sometimes the unravelling if she had made a mistake. Wool didn't always come in balls. Sometimes it was in skeins and we would sit with our arms outstretched with a great loop of wool as she pulled it out and rolled it into a ball. Numerous were the jumpers that my mother knitted and I would get them for birthdays or Christmas well into my middle age. I remember the wool made me itch and often they would shrink in the wash, but I would never not wear one she made. My sons also were a new reason to knit and I have many photographs of them wearing her creations. Happy times!

STAINBECK PREPARATORY SCHOOL

My first school was Stainbeck Preparatory School and it wasn't far from my grandmother's house in Chapel Allerton. My mother valued education and wanted the best for her sons. My elder brother had to change from a school near Oakwood that closed and somehow she found Stainbeck. I think there was a recommendation from one of her friends who lived in Ladywood near Oakwood. The school was small and was two old houses off Stainbeck Lane. It was owned by the Headmistress. I thought it was Mrs. Genge, but I have been told by a reader that she was a Miss. There was a uniform and it was a bright red blazer for the boys and a cap. The badge was a shield with interlocking letters SPS. I think the girls wore a dark blue pinafore dress in winter and a lighter check dress in summer. We had to change our shoes when we came in and named pumps were stored under the staircase. I started this school at four, which was a year earlier than most schools at the time. There was no playground, but a flat paved area at the back of the house and then a rockery that led down onto what would have been the garden. I remember there were some old apple trees. The lane, I think it is Bank View, that led down to the school was unpaved and there was a large hawthorn hedge on the left hand side and lovely big houses on the right. The school had high ceilings and a big staircase and in its day must have been quite a regal house. As a school, the floors were bare or linoleum-covered at best. Classes were small and I remember two teachers. One was Miss Cowling and she and I came to blows at one point and the other was Miss Blackmore. She was quite young for a teacher and I liked her. There was no space for gym or any other activities and we used to go out of the school up the hill a little, cross the road and use the small community hall for country dancing and other activities. Being my first school and having my older brother there, I loved it.

We were living up Easterly Road way at this time and we caught a bus down to Harehills and then had to catch another outside the Yorkshire Penny Bank that took us up the hill past Potternewton Park, past Chapel Allerton Hospital, to Chapel Allerton and then left onto Stainbeck Lane. It was quite a journey for an eight year old brother leading a four year old, but in these times there was no alternative. My mother needed to look after my younger brother, Stuart, and so we made the journey twice a day on our own. I was always a little scared of the double-decker buses with the open backs and when stressed I would have nightmares where I was on the bus and somehow I would be pulled towards the open back. It didn't matter how hard I held on to the bars, I was pulled nearer and nearer to the back and eventually off. This was the point I always woke up. My brother always did a good job looking after me and I don't think there was ever any problem. I loved the ticket machine and the big red bell buttons with a white surround that said 'press once'.

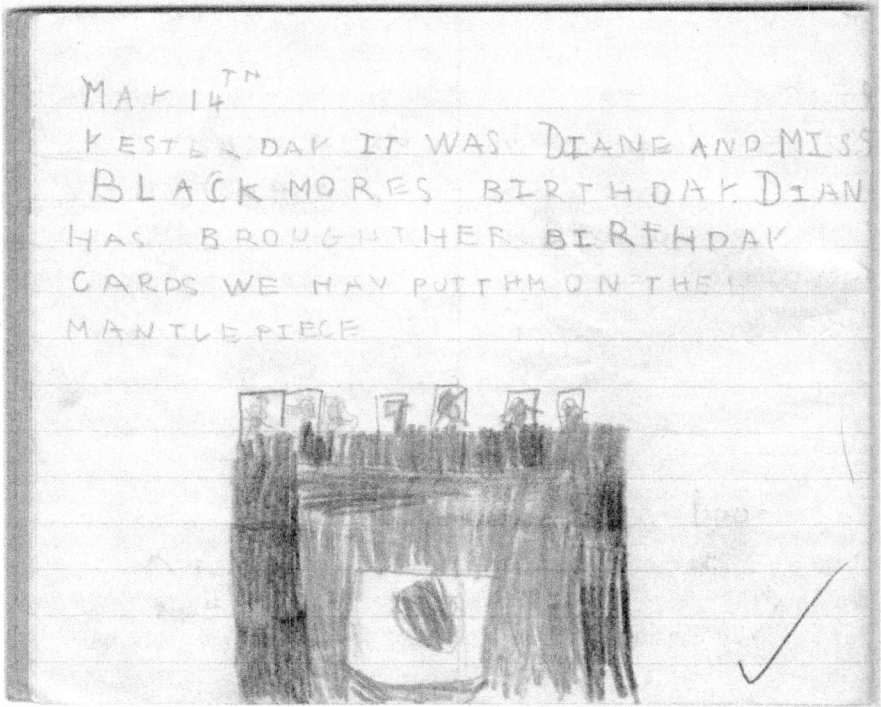

MAR 14TH
YESTERDAY IT WAS DIANE AND MISS
BLACKMORES BIRTHDAY DIAN
HAS BROUGHT HER BIRTHDAY
CARDS WE HAV PUT THM ON THE
MANTLEPIECE

I do remember learning to write and for some reason we were taught to write in block capitals and then cursive writing. We were never shown printing and I had to teach myself when I started working in schools many years later. I remember always writing my capital Ys backwards. Stories were wonderful and we learnt about Brer Rabbit, Aesop's Fables and my favourite, The Little Red Hen. I was given the book as a prize for learning to read. Janet and John was the popular reading scheme that is now frowned upon for its limited storylines. 'Run Janet run,' 'Run Spot run,' Run John run.' Maybe a little constricted in the art of the narrative, but it worked and I was captured by the written word. The joy of sharing your thoughts through words to other people is still an amazing process, and the mental images of a good writer are vivid and engaging. Teachers seemed to read stories a great deal at this time and Enid Blyton was popular. She did go out of vogue for many years, but has returned in the realisation that children loved them, and as part of generational nostalgia. The ones I loved the best were the Faraway Tree Stories.

One of my first memories is of going on a walk with the teacher out of the back of the school garden, along a lane to fields. We were told the fields belonged to Mr. Bean's farm. I am not sure if there was a Farmer Bean or whether it was a convenient name, but we looked at the hedgerows, the rich brown earth and when we returned to class we had to draw pictures of what we had seen and the class made a model on a painted board using toy farm animals, tractors and other

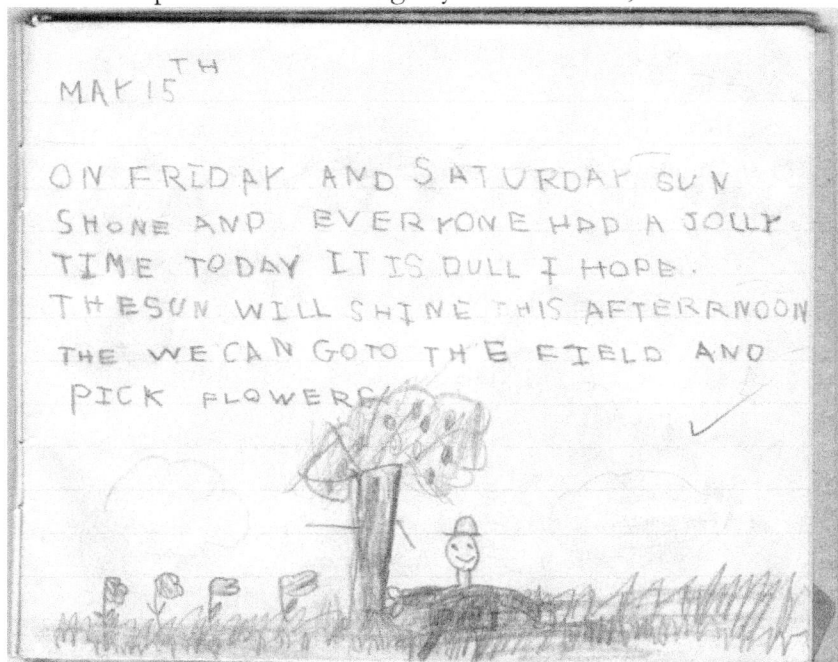

My book age six, 1961.

items to recreate the farm.

I only remember a couple of bad things happening at school and one was my run-in with Miss Cowling. At the start of the day as we entered school, we had to take our outside shoes off and put on our pumps. They didn't have laces and were the black slip-on ones. I got ready and we waited to go into the classroom. Miss Cowling was in a bit of a fluster as one girl couldn't find her pumps. She searched the collection of shoes under the stairs and for some reason decided that I had the wrong ones on. As a four year old, I was quite put out and indignant that I hadn't anyone else's pumps. I was told to take mine off, which I did angrily and threw them at the teacher. I am not sure who was more surprised, Miss Cowling or me! When she checked, they were mine, but I don't remember any apology, but I similarly don't remember any reprimand.

The second upsetting incident was getting my first exercise book. Prior to this, we had only used pieces of paper, but we must have been deemed good enough writers at this point to have an exercise book. The books were thin and had plain pages alternating with the lined pages. We were told to write our names on the cover, which I did. The mistake was that the books had no indication which was the front and which was the back and, as a result, I wrote my name on the back with the book upside down. The teacher I had then didn't worry, but I did. The book was covered to hide my mistake. This has stuck with me all my life, as has the book. I didn't realise it, but my mother kept that book and I still have it and I have scanned the evidence for public shaming.

I do remember one Christmas concert that we did. My elder brother and I were both in it, I believe. I can't remember too much, but we had to dress as red Indians. My father brought sacks home from Catton's Foundry for mum to turn into indian costumes. The sacks were washed and dyed brown and with a bit of work were turned into tunics with a belt of rope. We then had headbands and a feather. I do clearly recollect the uncomfortable nature of rough hessian sacks on the skin. They were very itchy and we both suffered for our art. The performance was in the evening and we were driven over to Stainbeck Road to a church hall, I think for, the concert.

My elder brother took his eleven plus four years before me and he left Stainbeck for high school. I stayed on until I was eight, but my time there was cut short by the sudden death of the headmistress and the subsequent closure of the school. For all its shortcomings as far as qualified teachers and facilities were concerned, the school had taught me to read, love learning and set me up for life. The last few years, from the age of five, I had had to travel on two buses to and from school on my own. This made me independent and confident and when Mr. Harold Wilson, the new head of Harehills County Primary asked me to read to him, and the only book he could find as he unpacked in his office on his first day was the Bible, I read with confidence and clarity. From this, Mr. Wilson placed me in the top class, much to my mother's relief. I believe a friend of mine from Stainbeck Prep School, Paul Banks, also started Harehills and eventually we both moved on to Roundhay School.

I was given an autograph book before I left Stainbeck Prep School and I remember Miss Blackmore signing it for me. She wrote 'a few lines from a poor poet' and then ruled three straight lines and signed it. As an eight year old, I didn't really understand it, but at least she did it for me, which made me happy.

STAINBECK PREPARATORY SCHOOL

Name David M. Cameron   Age 7yrs 7mths

Report for term ending July 19th   No. in Form 16

Average Age 7yrs 3mths

Form Pos.   Exam. Pos.   Conduct Good

SUBJECT	EXAM. %	REMARKS
Scripture	A	} Shows keen interest
History	A	
Geography	A	
Nature	A	
Literature		
Arithmetic	A	Very good
Tables	A	Very good
Mental Arithmetic	B+	Good
English	A	Good
Reading	A	Good
Dictation	B+	Good
Composition	A	Good imagination
Drawing	A	Very good
Phs. Culture		
General Knowledge	A	Very good

Principal's Remark : Very good progress indeed

Form II next term.

Next term begins on Sept. 4th

Form Mistress L E. Blackmore

Principal Radcliffe Senge

OPENING UP OF THE YORKSHIRE COUNTRYSIDE.

It seems strange nowadays, but when I was born in the 1950s, most families did not own cars. Transport was public and it meant utilising trains, trams, buses and coaches to get anywhere. One of the results of this was that travelling to and from places had to be planned and it was a much more time consuming endeavour. The idea of just dropping by to visit a friend or relative on a whim was almost unheard of.

In early memories, I have covered the original car that the family owned and I believe it was one of the first in the street, if not the first. Even if your family owned a car their reliability was not what it is today. The old Austin A7 Ruby, known as the 'Fridge' as it had no heating and was started with a crank handle, meant any trip in it was a real challenge as it was prone to breaking down. I do remember one outing to the North Yorkshire Moors, Fylingdales just south of Whitby. It was where there was an RAF base that had the Early Warning System for a nuclear attack. The

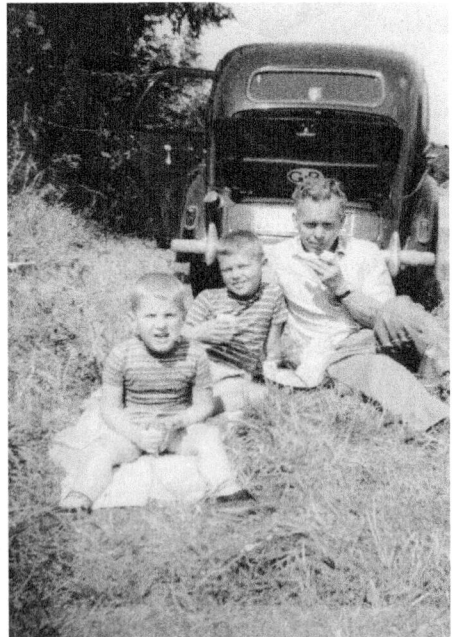

Ford Prefect. Dad and older brother Andrew.

detectors were in structures that looked like giant white golf balls. You could see them from the little road that cut through the moors, but you were well away from it as there was a fence and warning signs of terrible things that might happen to you if you entered. Apparently, it would provide a four minute warning, which was probably sufficient time for Britain to send its missiles off to devastate the USSR as it was then. We had arranged to go on the trip with my aunty and uncle. They went in their car and we followed along in ours. Their car must have been newer and more reliable. All was going well until we hit the steep hills getting up to the moor.

Austin A7 Ruby.

The 'Fridge' failed to live up to its name and started to overheat. We all pulled over to the side of the road and had a picnic whilst Dad and Uncle Ernest checked the car. I don't think that there was much that could be done, except allow it to cool and then carry on. Anyway, we managed to see the day out, but its unreliability led to it being replaced with the Ford Prefect. This was a larger car, shiny, with running boards and certainly more reliable. Of course, seat belts did not exist in these times and the dashboards were hard metal and would have provided little protection if there were an accident. Starting was always a challenge and the choke would be pulled out, there would be a tense wait as the engine would turn once, twice and hopefully start on the third turn.

The Prefect allowed us to venture out into the Yorkshire countryside on day trips and it would have been at this time that tourism began and scenic parts of the country started to attract sightseers. Before this, it would have been coach trips, but these would have mostly been to seaside towns or larger centres. Cars allowed working folk to go to new and exciting places that trains and buses didn't venture to. Fountains Abbey near Ripon, Brimham Rocks near Harrogate, Plumpton Rocks, Knaresborough, Harrogate, Otley Chevin, The Cow and Calf at Ilkley and the most magnificent, Malham Cove, all became available and the beauty of the Yorkshire countryside could be enjoyed and appreciated.

I must admit that there was the added excitement and tension about the early trips. The Prefect was only slightly more reliable than the 'Fridge' and so there was that added spice of not knowing whether you would get to your destination, or whether you would get home without the car breaking down. Add to this the noise and chaos of at first two boys and later three carrying on and falling out in the back seats, one of whom suffered travel sickness. My father would never stop, whether it was to let my brother out, ask for directions, or to give our legs a stretch. My mother would be the map reader, and the pilot and navigator were never in agreement. Oh, the joys of it all! We did sing a lot. Sometimes it would be endless green bottles or we might play games like I Spy, as there were no car radios in these times and certainly no IPads.

One trip has stuck with me all my life and it illustrates my parents' relationship and the etiquette of the time. We went to Brimham Rocks and if you have never been, you have never lived, as my father was wont to say. It is a fabulous place and, as boys, we were in heaven. Sculptured and weathered boulders covered the area in an alien landscape of endless possibilities: climbing, hiding, finding caves and holes, as well as the ubiquitous picnic with thermos flask of tea, egg sandwiches and biscuits. The journey was a longer one as the roads were narrow and the Ford Prefect was not built for great speed. Sabot (the Wonder Dog as someone called him) was in the back with us and we arrived incident free. There were quite a lot of other people there as the weather was good and it was quite a hot day. Dad pulled off the road amongst the rocks and stopped in a little grassy bit. We piled out the back, excited, when there was a cry from my mother in the front. In the hurry of getting everything packed and ready, she had forgotten to change from her slippers. My dad's response was 'Oh, Peggy! Well, you can't get out like that!" Nowadays, I am sure we wouldn't bat an eyelid and would have either gone barefoot or wearing fluffy slippers, but in these times it would have been a major embarrassment. The result was a real dampener on the trip. Mum stayed in the car. She did open the door and held Sabot on the lead. The rest of us sat on the tartan picnic blanket and had the picnic as usual, but there was a definite mood and silence as my mother had let my father down. Needless to say, we didn't stay all that long and, as you can guess, it never happened again.

Grandma and Grandad Cameron at the cottage at Oban.

One of our more regular journeys was to Ilkley. Now there were two reasons for this. The first was that Ilkley Moors are fantastic and the Cow and Calf well worth a visit, and the second was that we had relatives there. My grandfather on the Scottish side and my Aunty Chris lived there. Chris had two children and they owned a shop on the main street. I think it was called Scots' House and it sold Scottish clothing. The two cousins were older than my brothers and me and there was a boy and a girl. The house was multi-storeyed above the shop and was very big. My male cousin had an enormous Scalextric in the attic and an air-rifle range in the cellar. This was almost unheard of for anyone I knew, so we loved to go and play there.

My grandfather was from Oban, Scotland, and he was originally a gamekeeper. There was my Aunty Chris, my dad and another uncle called Jim. Jim was an academic at St Andrew's University. My father had been in the submarines during the Second World War, on HMS Scotsman as Chief Petty Officer and he was an engineer. He moved to Leeds after the war to work at Catton's Steel Foundry on Black Bull Street. For some reason which I have never discovered, my grandfather left my grandmother behind in Scotland and came to live with his daughter, my Aunty Chris, in Ilkley. He was a bit serious as a grandfather and not at all like Harry and Mary Wray in Chapel Allerton, who were so open and loving. He did come and stay with us in Gipton Wood Crescent for a week and we would go on walks to the Soldiers' Field at Oakwood. I remember well, large flocks of sea gulls that were feeding and they would take flight at our approach or the intrusion of over-eager dogs. On these walks I was amazed at how he could find coins on the ground as we walked. My grandfather seemed to be constantly looking down and picking up pennies, threepences or sixpences and he would present us with them. I was staggered at how clever he was and how careless people must be. It was only as an adult that I realised what he was doing. It was his way of giving us some pocket money without it being overt.

The car trips to Ilkley became something that my dad and us would do without mum. There was some sort of family falling out that I didn't and don't know the cause of, so mum didn't come along on the visits. I remember the final straw as we broke down once again just before we got to Otley. It was shortly after this that we got our first new car. I think it was bought from Brown and Whites and it was a Ford Anglia, the one with the inward sloping rear window. It was an almost greeny, duck-egg blue and my younger brother recently let me know the registration number, AUG277C, which was quite easy to learn. To say it was a major improvement would have been an understatement. It started first time, it was reliable and it wasn't black, which was quite a change. Henry Ford said that you could have any colour as long as it was black, but things changed in the 1960s. That car and the ones that followed took us all over Yorkshire and then up to Scotland once to see my dad's home near Oban and we even managed Bournemouth and Torquay, where you could go in the sea for more than a few seconds without your feet turning blue. The arrival of cars provided the masses with opportunities that they could never have dreamt of, much as package holidays and cheap flights did for the following generation. We didn't realise how lucky we were!

STARTING HAREHILLS COUNTY PRIMARY SCHOOL

Harehills County Primary School

I can't say that I didn't enjoy my time at Harehills CP School. Apart from the caretaker sending me to see Mr Wilson for chasing around the cloakroom, they were some of the happiest times of my life. Compared to Stainbeck Preparatory School which was so homely and quaint, Harehills seemed enormous. Classes were large and the primary school probably had about three-hundred children. The school consisted of the infants school, which I never attended and the primary school that was on the right hand side and the level above. There were two playgrounds and our primary one consisted of a sloping, walled, tarmac covered yard, with the caretaker's house in the corner. School caretakers used to live on the grounds in these times and I suppose it meant that there was someone keeping an eye on the premises twenty four hours a day and seven days a week. They all disappeared when I started teaching, which was a shame and probably led to an increase in vandalism and break-ins. I am not sure that the caretaker or his wife would have enjoyed their walls being used as the cricket stumps or the soccer goals, but maybe they just got used to the constant thumping during morning and lunch breaks. For the first couple of years, the toilets were outside and fairly dire. They were bitterly cold in winter and not places you would want to linger. They replaced them after a year or two and I think the new ones were a temporary building and certainly an improvement. The entire school was structurally suspect though and this was probably the reason it was demolished. We were told that the hall floor upstairs wasn't strong enough to hold an audience of parents seated on chairs, which meant we didn't have concerts where parents could attend. I remember very well being asked to come out of Mr Kelly's class and to jump up and down on the hall floor whilst surveyors measured the movement. Again, I am not sure that children would be used as guinea pigs nowadays.

Regardless of all the school's faults, I and the other children didn't care. It was our school and it offered a world of opportunities and you just got used to lining up, marching across the crossing and down the road to have lunch in the hall under St Aiden's Church, getting onto to double-decker buses to go for sport on the Soldiers' Field, changing on the bus or in the classroom and I think walking to swimming, through Potternewton Park. It was just part of our everyday experience. I had loved Stainbeck Prep and I loved Harehills. In those days, it was full of interesting things that had their own season, or you experienced as you moved through the school.

My first class had metal double desks which were heavy and immovable, but these were replaced by more modern ones. I remember the time that we got ink pens. It was a major milestone and was full of mystery and special utensils. Inkwells had a large hole at the top of the desk and the little pots had to be topped up with ink on a regular basis. Only the most trusted became inkwell monitors. The ink had to be mixed with water and any ink on your fingers seemed to remain forever. The pens were bare wooden dowel, with a metal clip that held the nibs. The first time we got one it was special. I don't think they were ever new, but that didn't really matter. The nibs were new, at least for the first day and they were bright shiny, silvery, sharp and pointed. The pointed end was split and there was a hole half way down the nib where the ink collected and flowed along the split as you added pressure. The watery ink took a long time to dry and we were issued with small squares of blotting paper. Writing with the pens was an acquired skill and it took a lot of practice to avoid tearing the paper, smudging the writing or blotting your work. It must have been hell for left-handed children as their hand would pass over the fresh writing as they wrote. In these days there weren't many allowances made for left-handers and in Catholic Schools being left-handed, **sinister** (in Latin), was seen as the work of the Devil. The Devil sat at the left of us all and hence salt was thrown over the left shoulder into the eye of the Devil, if it was spilt. Children would be chastised if they used their left hands, regardless of whether that was their natural side. That didn't happen at Harehills, at least not when I was there, but I don't remember any left-handed scissors or the like.

We had special books that our parents had to buy where there were exercises for us to practise and copy the cursive style. One thing about Stainbeck Preparatory School was that I was taught to write using block capitals as my four exercise books that my mother kept show, and this meant I had no idea how to print and in fact it was a skill I had to learn as an adult when I became a teacher. At Harehills, we learned to write Cursive handwriting and as a result I was never taught or learned to print. We were taught how to hold a pen correctly, how to use the blotting paper to dry the ink and how to use the correct pressure to avoid blotting. Of course, there was a wide variety of skill levels in the class and some unfortunate children did feel Mr Kelly's wrath and his famous, "Angels and Ministers of Grace Defend Us!" phrase he would use when exasperated.

The classroom had bare, rough floorboards and we soon got the skill of using the pens as darts. Thrown with the right amount of force and direction we could get them to stick in the floorboards and they would wobble, just like Robin Hood's arrows would do in a castle doorway. Of course this didn't do the nibs much good and the ends would become crossed and prove difficult to write with. We bent them back into shape, but they were never as good again until finally we plucked up courage to ask Mr Kelly for new ones. If we found him in a good mood then we would return to our desks with a replacement. If he wasn't, then there would be a public dressing down on the ability to look after school property, before we were allowed to return to our places shame-faced in front of the class.

The other use for our writing equipment was the making of blotting paper and ink balls. If the paper was soaked with ink then it could be rolled into a soggy ball of indigo and then we could either flick the balls at other children sitting around us, or if it was pea shooter season, blow the balls of paper and ink at the back of the heads of children sitting in front of you. The pea shooters could be bought from the tobacconist/sweetshop across the road from the school. We would get dried peas from home, and the tubes of metal had a cone of plastic mouthpiece. They were about eight inches long and you placed the ammunition in the hole at the mouthpiece and with a sharp, powerful blow sent the pea shooting out with force. The hard peas could be quite painful, but in the instance of blotting paper balls, there was no pain, just and indigo stain on the head, face or hair. The one thing that was essential was to be fully aware of what the teacher was doing. It would have been more than your life was worth to be caught and so we tended to wait until Mr Kelly left the room. It only took a moment for warfare to break out as numerous pea shooters would appear, be loaded and the projectiles fired. We would wait all day, maybe even two or more before the opportunity arose, but it was well worth the wait.

I mentioned that most toys had a season and I think this was because eventually, marbles, whip'n'tops, pea shooters etc would be banned at school. I assume that Mr Wilson or Mr Kelly would have had a word at the shop to ask them not to sell them and so they disappeared before returning the next season. Of course I didn't realise this at the time. It is only with adult, teacher eyes, that I realise what was going on.

The use of the dip pens disappeared during the second year that I was in Mr Kelly's class. New ball point pens were introduced. These were primary coloured pens that tapered towards each end. They were about pencil length and with their arrival something sad happened as the dip pens and all the ritual vanished overnight. The ink monitors and equipment, as well as the skills we had honed were replaced and the modern world impinged. Technology made dip pens obsolete and the history from quills to the school dip pen ended. Mr Kelly even showed us how to make a dip pen using a large feather and he used his pen-knife to cut and split a nib. Technological advancement has brought many wonderful blessings, but it does come at a cost and I am sure that there are others who look back fondly on the simple times we grew up in. I guess every generation feels this.

BAGATELLE AND OTHER GAMES

Andrew and me as a toddler.

I was trying to think about some of games that we played when we were little in the late 1950s, early 60s and one that came to mind that I have not mentioned was Bagatelle. For those who are unsure what this is, I suppose it was the non-electronic origin of the Pinball machine. It consisted of a flat board about a yard long and twenty inches or so wide. There was a spring mechanism that would fire marbles into the game board and the purpose was to gain as many points as possible by landing in nailed targets, but the most points came from the small indented concave areas.

You fired your marbles, usually six, and then you added up your score and then the other player, or players took their turns. The skill was in the amount of pressure you put on the spring trigger. You pulled the plunger back and then released it. Too much pressure and the marble would tend to miss everything and land at the bottom without scoring. Too little force and it would either roll back down the firing lane or just exit onto the board and again roll to the bottom without scoring. You did get another go if it fell back down the firing lane.

It was a very simple game and I am sure that many of them were home-made. The patterns of the nails and targets seemed very similar and if any of the nails fell out it was really easy to repair. I believe Andrew got one for Christmas one year. It certainly wasn't new, but no one cared, and we all got a great deal of fun out of it. It was one of those things that all the family could have a go at, much like the card games that families would sit around and play.

Cards were very popular. They were inexpensive, offered a range from the simplest of games such as Snap, through to the most complex such as Bridge. Adults would play cards at home and often in the pub, where Cribbage, with its board and matchsticks, was popular. At home, apart from Snap, we loved Happy Families. Who could forget Mr. Bun the Baker and the host of other families and occupations? Even if you didn't want to play card games you could always make towers out of the cards. Towards the end of the fifties home-life was changing dramatically. Originally, families would listen to the radio for entertainment or sing around the piano, but TV had started just in time for the Queen's Coronation and families began to see the breakdown of the need to entertain themselves.

Another of the games that we loved was Dominoes. It was a game that you could play at whatever age and adults would play in the pubs where betting was often involved. At home, we might sometimes have played for pennies, particularly with grandma in Chapel Allerton. There didn't seem to be the political correctness that dominates current society nowadays and I suppose it was a way of Grandma giving us a few pennies to buy some sweets. The other additional attraction of dominoes was that you could set them all up and knock the first one down and watch, mesmerised, as they all toppled in turn.

One Christmas I was given a train set. It was second-hand from next door and it was set on a wooden board. It was hidden, not very well, behind the settee in the front room. I had seen it since it was first put there, but I was shrewd enough not to mention it. When Christmas came and I got it, I learnt about the drama there was just before the big day. The locomotive wouldn't work and so my dad had had to rush out to buy a new one. In these more affluent times that wouldn't be such a big deal but then it was an expense they hadn't planned for.

The locomotive was a Hornby and it was black and shiny. I didn't care whether the set was new or not. I loved it! I added things to it over time. You could get little houses and stations and I remember building a tunnel and buying artificial bushes to set it off. I didn't have a lot, but it allowed my imagination to run riot and I could get lost. The train was controlled by a transformer and there was a knob to increase speed, both forwards and backwards. I never became a big train fanatic, but I enjoyed it and just once I went with a friend train-spotting, but I can't say I was impressed. The age of steam was fast disappearing and the diesel trains didn't have the same magic.

At various times I was given Meccano and I had great fun with it. It was quite challenging to make models using tiny nuts and bolts and using small spanners and screwdrivers, but it was great for developing patience and dexterity. The metal plates, green or red, had perforated holes and, depending on the kit, you could make all sorts of things. I believe I had one that made a car with a steering wheel mechanism that turned the front wheels. Some kits made cranes that had a hook and by turning a handle you could lower and raise objects. Both my elder brother and I had some and I think you could even get electric winches for them, but that could just be my wishful thinking. Meccano disappeared for many years, but has made a comeback and we bought a set for my grandson.

Other construction kits were available and I had one with a plastic base and there were prefabricated plastic panels that fitted onto thin metal bars. You could add doors, window frames and roofs to build a range of houses and buildings. I cannot remember the name, but it lost out to the major winner, Lego. A boy three houses down in Gipton Wood Crescent, I think the family were the Chances (so my brother Andrew informs me), had the most Lego we had ever seen.

He had a big box of hundreds of pieces. I used to love going round to play. We didn't follow plans to build specific projects, we just let our imaginations run wild. We would make spaceships and have battles, or build the tallest towers we could manage before they would finally topple and fall into a myriad of pieces. We would fashion pistols and ray guns and we would chase each other around the house. It was a great time, but the noise must have been horrendous. His mother was always patient and I never saw her get into a state. I think he had three sisters, so boys in the house would have come as a shock. We were often sent into the garden and there they had a wonderful wooden cubby house (den) built by their dad. It was strong enough to climb on the roof and the base was dug below the soil level, so it was always damp, but we loved it. I don't think they had much of a garden as we would have destroyed any attempt at keeping plants growing. One thing they did have was the largest white rabbit I have ever seen. It was kept in a hutch at the back of the garage and when they went on holiday we would have the task of keeping it fed and watered. Now you would think this would be an easy task, but then you never met the rabbit! For some reason, it could sense you approaching the hutch and, on signal, it would cock its leg and squirt a stream of urine at you. That rabbit never missed! You could attempt a sly creeping up, or a mad dash, but whatever you tried it was up to the challenge and would get you. It was just the same with my elder brother and so you could imagine the arguments we had about whose turn it was to change the food and water. I had forgotten all about this until I started writing, so I apologise for the digression.

One game that I only ever played at other people's houses was Magic Robot. It was a general knowledge quiz game where the question was selected on one board and then a plastic robot with a metal wand was fitted. You would turn the robot until the wand pointed to the question. The robot was then removed and it was placed in the answer circle. The robot would turn until the wand pointed to the answer. Magic or at least science. It fascinated me at the time, but now would be very easy to explain.

Other games that came into vogue for Christmas or birthday presents were things like Etch-A-Sketch. By turning the two knobs, simple drawings could be made. They could be removed by shaking the game. It seemed a bit of a development of a cheap cardboard drawing game, which had a clear plastic layer over a sticky backing. You drew with a stylus and a dark line appeared. To clear the picture you just pulled the top layer of plastic up from the bottom, removing it from the sticky backing and you could start again. I have just checked and Etch-A-Sketch is still available and still popular.

As I got a little older then board games became a focus. Christmas would often see compendium of games, like draughts, chess, Ludo and snakes and ladders. These were good fun and with an older brother and a growing younger brother we began to play without adults. Monopoly had become hugely successful and my family would play. There were a lot of social skills involved and probably the biggest challenge was learning to lose.

My brother Andrew had a friend, David Musgrove, and he lived on Easterly Road and they had a new board game called Risk. I was invited to go with my brother to David's house and he allowed his brother, Richard, to play. The four of us would spend hours in their box room, dominating the world and each other. It is probably one of the nastiest games ever, as pacts were formed and broken in a bid to finally take over the world. It did introduce some basic geography and so I learnt where many of the main countries were. I became quite friendly with Richard and he later invited me to join his Scout group.

There was one game that became a real hit in the sixties, particularly with teenagers or those soon to be, and that was Twister. This game provided an opportunity to contort your body over and under those you were playing with and was a source of great mirth. The spinning of a wheel then directed which colour you had to place your hand or foot on. This was fun at Christmas parties and my grandma would have a go, much to everyone's delight, and she wasn't afraid to hitch up her dress and expose her voluminous knickers. We did laugh!

'TRYERS' BADGES'

As I have said before, I loved Harehills C.P. School, and I think it was my experience there that set me on the road to becoming a teacher and spending my working life dealing with children, staff and parents

One of Mr. Harold Wilson's innovations was the 'tryers' badges'. These were red felt shields, with a safety pin at the back. They were awarded one to each class for the child that had tried the hardest to achieve, behave, or some other worthy cause and were presented in assembly each Friday. Mr. Wilson was being quite progressive for these times as stars were awarded for achievement, charts showing how students were behaving and points for houses were the norm. It was a time of dog-eat-dog: students were ranked for every subject and streamed by ability, so recognition of non-academic merit was something new. I don't think Mr. Kelly was too keen on this as he would look at the register and ask who hadn't received one that term or year and then choose one at random. Maybe he thought the top class didn't need them to motivate themselves. Anyway, I do know that I was always delighted when I received mine in assembly.

The opposite to the badges was corporal punishment and I do remember witnessing children being slippered for some misdemeanour or other. Usually it was a gym shoe, 'pump' as they were known, sometimes modified by removing almost all the shoe but the sole, and this had the effect of producing a very impressive 'THWACK!', without too much discomfort. I do remember being told to attend a teacher's classroom after lunch for not lining up properly. I don't know the teacher's name, but it was one of the lower

Harehills CP Choir 1966 - Me third from right, back row. (Uniform only for the choir)

Year Four classes, to the left of the stage and behind it. There was a very long list and we marched forward, bent over and got an almighty whack with a blackboard ruler, one of the wide ones, and then we marched back to our classes. I can only think he was a young teacher who was struggling with a difficult class and thought discipline and respect came from fear. He was definitely wrong, but they were different times. I also remember one or two being slippered, I don't think caned, on stage, in front of the school. I can only think this was for something very serious as it had a big impression on me, and I'm sure on them. At Roundhay School though, it was very common, but I was never caned. Slippered, yes, and slapped in the face by a teacher, but never caned. I guess my teenage smirk and attitude were too much to bear for the maths teacher who slapped me!

On a lighter note, I do remember in Mr. Kelly's class making pin-hole cameras. I believe that there was to be an eclipse and it was too dangerous to look with the naked eye, so we made boxes with a tracing paper sheet at the back. By putting a small hole at the front you could make a pinhole camera that allowed light to pass onto the sheet of tracing paper and if pointed at the eclipse, you could safely look at the small image on the tracing paper without harming your eyes. On the day of the eclipse, at about two in the afternoon, we traipsed out into the playground to point the cameras at the sun and be thoroughly disappointed by the tiny image of the eclipse.

Another time, I also remember him informing us that he was going to bring in a cow's eye to dissect the next day, as part of science and on another occasion it was a heart. This was far more interesting and we watched as he struggled to cut a slimy large eye with a safety razor blade. It was hard going, but in the end he managed, removed the lens, showed us the vitreous humour and disgusted some of the girls, but certainly captured the attention of most of the boys. The heart dissection was similarly gory, but we saw valves and learnt about the basic structure.

It was about this time that I bought a book that is still available in a very modified form today. 365 Things to Do in Science and Nature, was quite a hefty book, with an experiment a day for eager scientists to carry out. I must add a note here. Most of the experiments are now banned for safety reasons as they involved poisonous or explosive substances, or things that now are illegal. How to blow wild birds' eggs is no longer thought of as an acceptable pastime. Taxidermy is not something a ten year old should be carrying out, particularly on the family pet or the old aunt, but it was in the book. Crystal growing is fine, but all the chemicals suggested are now recognised as unsuitable as they are poisonous. Potassium Permanganate, Copper Sulphate and others worked brilliantly, but are not in primary chemistry sets. Neither are magnesium ribbon or phosphorous, for obvious reasons. Similarly, much that we did at high school is no longer permitted. Pouring mercury around the desk is rather frowned on in these safety conscious days.

One thing I did enjoy though, was the choir and also the recorders. I remember taking the note home that asked parents' permission to buy a recorder. I believe they were five shillings, but I can hardly believe they would be that much. My mum signed the note, provided me with the money and Mr. Kelly collected it the next morning and the order went in. Now, the creation of the recorder is clear proof that the Devil does exist. No benign God would allow such an instrument of torture to be created. After forty years in schools, I can still wake in the early hours of the morning shuddering with the memory of a class of children playing recorders. The descant is by far the worst. It reaches a pitch that even dogs can't hear and makes the scraping of finger nails on a blackboard seem like a wonderful melody.

With only a few holes and supposedly tuned, no one prepared me for the onslaught of a class of ten year olds blowing like their lives depended on it, whilst being shown how to place the fingers to make note C. I now realise why Mr. Kelly's hair was white! Eventually we, or at least some of us, improved. A recorder group of the less ham-fisted and ventilatingly challenged, were chosen and we would play for school sometimes in assemblies. Choir was similarly selected. During my time in teaching, any child wishing to join the choir had to be accommodated, but in those days careful selection was made to separate the wheat from the chaff. I wonder how many were emotionally scarred for life as a result of not being selected? Choir had to perform at some out of hours concerts and we had to wear a white shirt and red tie. I have always loved singing and somehow I slipped through the vetting process. We also did a children's operetta called something like, 'Storyland'. Some children had quite big solos and I had one line. I still remember it well. The cast introduced their characters and I had to sing, 'I'm Aladdin and not a sham'. This was followed by someone singing, 'I'm old King Cole, Ho! Ho!' Everyone then came in with the chorus of, 'Storyland is both wide and fair, everybody can travel there, big folk and little folk think it's grand. Stor -y-land, Stor-y-land!' Oh, what fun!

Another aspect of schooling in these times was the Eleven Plus. This selection test was designed to separate those for an academic education from those who would pursue a future technical or practical education. For many parents, passing the tests and being offered a place at a grammar school was a measure of their success, whereas I don't remember being too phased about it. Friday in Mr Kelly's class was test practice day and parents were asked to buy Progress Papers Books in Maths, English and General Knowledge. On Fridays, we would do one of each of the tests from the books to prepare us for the Eleven Plus test. I enjoyed doing them and luckily for most in Mr. Kelly's class they were in a similar position. On the days of the actual eleven plus testing, all the fourth year did the test in the hall. Chairs and desks were arranged in rows and were facing the front in alphabetical order. When instructed, we opened the booklets and worked our way through them. Afterwards, we all gathered and discussed how we had done. Because of the streaming, we were unaware of how some children were stressed and when the results came out almost all of our class were chosen for grammar school and a handful from the next class down, but the majority were not selected and were sent to a range of Secondary Modern and Comprehensive schools. I was pleased to be going to Roundhay School as that was where most of my friends were going, but really had no understanding of how that would impact on my life or other children's.

FUN AND GAMES

Today I am taken back to the game seasons that we enjoyed. Modern children may not experience the simple pleasures that we had and I suppose necessity was definitely the mother of invention. At various times throughout the school year, there were quite definite 'seasons' for games that we could play on the tarmac playground. The lack of space didn't seem to be a problem and in the warmer months cricket was played with chalked wickets on the caretaker's house or the back wall near the toilet blocks. The slope added to the local challenge. Winter would see soccer as the main boys' sport, but the girls seemed occupied with a variety of games such as skipping, hopscotch, cat's cradle and handstands against the walls. The thought of skull fractures didn't seem to worry anyone at that time. Nowadays, health and safety would have put an end to it.

On frosty days we made ice slides, and with the polishing of many feet on the ice, these could be whipped up to high speed slides that allowed trains of children to hurtle down the ice and often ended in pile-ups. We would start these from the moment we arrived at school, and if we were lucky, they would still be there at morning break time for us to continue. Sometimes, adult concern led to ashes being spread to prevent further use and accidents. The killjoys! I have a recollection of occasionally being able to slide from the top of the yard all the way down to the far wall near the 'bogs'. The ecstasy of balancing, rugged up in scarf and hat, running pell-mell and then gliding, arms akimbo, has stayed with me all my life. Those boys and girls who could show their prowess had real kudos and the younger children would watch, idolise and aim to achieve such greatness.

Even some of the teachers seemed to watch on with admiration and occasionally the young staff even had a go.

Sliding on the ice and general soccer and playing could destroy shoes in next to no time. My mother always bought me Tuff Shoes as they came with a six month, no quibble, guarantee. Due to the way I played on the tarmac they never lasted above five or six weeks and each time a hole appeared we went back and got a new pair. This went on for several years before they decided that they would only exchange them once. I also remember soaking wet feet in winter due to the holes and the pipes in the classrooms were a smelly, steaming array of socks, gloves and scarves. We learnt quickly the dangers of putting frozen hands on the pipes as 'chilblains', agonising stimulation of the nerves, would result. I never had good circulation and my brothers and I have hands that seize up in cold weather.

Andrew, younger brother Stuart and me in the garden at Lawrence Avenue.

I do remember one specific morning when the playground was covered in thick snow. This was fairly uncommon, but on this occasion snowmen were made and two forts, with ice walls, as bases. Snow balls were created, stored and all hell was let loose for short bursts. No one was safe and some of the snowballs became ice and really hurt if you were hit in the face. The ice melted a bit with all the heavy foot traffic, but enough remained for us to continue at the break and was still there at lunch. One or two unwary children were struck in the face and there were some bloody mouths and tear soaked faces. The wise learnt to keep an eye in the back of the head. It was glorious!

Spring would arrive eventually and so did 'whip 'n' top' season. For the uninitiated, a 'whip 'n' top' consisted of a usually green wooden stick with a leather thong, the whip, and a wooden pinecone-shaped grooved top with a metal point. You would wrap the thong around the top and then, holding the top, loosely tug the whip back. This sent the top spinning and the knack was to keep the top spinning, with repeated whips. It was a definite skill and some became masters. I was a player, but not a leader in this. 'Whip 'n' tops' could only be purchased during the season and the sweet shop directly across the zebra crossing outside school had a supply. When the season was on, you had to get in early to avoid disappointment as demand could become huge. I suppose scores of children whipping away at the tops was probably quite a sight and also quite a danger, but we all survived.

There were also two other major seasons. In the autumn we had conkers! Conkers, the seeds of the horse chestnut tree were beautiful, tactile nuts. At this time, children went on expeditions to gather their stash for the season. Some had the old faithful trees that they returned to each year, whilst others sought pastures new for richer pickings. I tended to return to old sites, but early plundering could have decimated my usual harvest and a bike ride further afield became a necessity. When fully ripe, the nuts would fall from their green, mine-like spiky cases. They would just lie scattered beneath the large spreading trees: shiny, brown, like polished eggs of wood. However, such finds were rare as someone would have already gathered the booty. On these occasions, drastic action was called for and sticks would be thrown up at the conkers that could be seen still in the trees. When we were successful we would dart in and prise open the shell, examine the creamy white velvet soft inside and discover whether we had a 'beauty' or not. I would experience the same excitement and anticipation as a Japanese pearl diver would as they opened the oyster shell to see if a pearl hid inside. Often my satchel would be full of the shiny, tactile harvest and I would cycle home with joy, pride and contentment.

Conkers is a very English pastime. A hole would be bored through the conker and a shoelace threaded through, aglet first. A knot would then be tied and you were ready. Two children would present with their conkers to challenge each other to a duel to the death. One would suspend his or her conker and the other would position themselves to have a 'shot' at it. This meant winding the lace or string around your finger, holding the conker and flicking it at the other. If you hit, you had another go. This would continue until you missed. At this point the opponent took their turn. The object was to knock your opponent's conker off their string or break it in two. In fact, there was the same chance of winning either holding your conker up or being the shooter, but you never could tell. Sometimes bits would fly off, but as long as some remained on the lace you were still in the game.

Now anyone who was a 'conkerer', would know that there were not quite legal ways to skew things in your favour. The obvious one was choice of conker. Size may not matter in many things, but it did in the conker world. Mass meant longevity and a well-proportioned conker could live to fight may battles before succumbing. Other tactics, whispered behind hands in the corner of the yard or classroom, involved soaking them in vinegar, drying them out or baking them. I have tried all of the above and some, that I am sworn to secrecy about, but I can't say that any really made much of a difference.

The games often resulted in bruised hands and knuckles and numerous accusations of cheating. In those days, you sorted out your own problems and teachers rarely intervened. I wish it had been so during my tenure as a headmaster, but alas it was not to be!

The other major 'season' was marbles and it was possible to have more than one marble season in some years. The marble craze helped supplement the local shops and there was a great run on marbles. Winners from previous years would have tins full that they had won off luckless children, whilst the novices sported small amounts of pristine marbles with crystal clear glass outers. During the season, large numbers of small clusters of children could be found huddled at their favourite spots in the yard. A hollow was used and the object was to win all of the marbles by striking opponents into the hollow. The rules were complex and there were a range of calls and tactics, that I can no longer remember, but victori sunt spolia, (to the victor the spoils) and you knew to avoid anyone with a large tin of marbles, as their skill was proven. Different size and coloured marbles had various names and value, but that has slipped my mind over the years. Someone may still own the wisdom and law of the ancient game, as played at Harehills C. P. School and be prepared to re-enlighten us geriatric practitioners.

Minor games were played at times such as 'Jacks', but again I don't have the same memories of this. What has come to me whilst I write this is something that nowadays would be outlawed, but was particularly popular with the boys. There were two sorts of cards collected. Probably these were different years, but there were American Civil War Cards and Mars Attacks Cards. The American Civil War ones were first, I think, and came with facsimile US dollars of the time. They even got on the news as some people thought they were authentic. The cards came with bubble gum and they were truly the most violent and gruesome things I have ever seen. Impaling, bayonetting was graphically shown in pictures and children would collect great packs of them and swap them. Parents didn't seem concerned in any way and, at the time, cowboy films were all the rage and we always played Cowboys and Indians and scalped any captives. Maybe they were right, parents that is, as we didn't grow up scalping and impaling. The second set of cards showed the invasion of Martians and again the pictures were chilling with their ferocity and violence. I guess that some things have improved since then and I won't dwell on them any more.

Last night something someone mentioned reminded me of the Harehills C.P. School song. I still remember the tune and we used to sing it at assemblies. The school motto was 'Aim High' and below is my recollection of the first verse. I hope it brings back fond memories.

> Amidst the busy streets of Leeds
> For years a school has stood
> A symbol of the children's needs
> Rejoicing in their golden deeds
> A power for doing good
> So let us sing our song on high
> Look up Harehills
> Harehills aim high!
>
> **(Harehills C.P. School Song)**

SWEETS, INKWELLS AND APPLES.

The sweetshop across the road from the school was Ashworth's and another reminded me of frozen Jubblies, so I thought I'd better delve into the wonderful world of sweets, or lollies, as they are called here in Perth, Western Australia.

The shop across from Harehills C.P. School was a treasure trove for a young boy with just a little bit of money to spend. The shop bell would sound as you entered into a world that childhood dreams were made of. In those days there was little that you could pick up and handle. Sweets were stored behind the counter in glass jars with screw tops. They offered a cornucopia of tantalising tastes to young palates. The whole process of asking for two ounces of aniseed balls and then standing, whilst the shopkeeper found the correct jar, screwed the lid off, poured an amount into the silver pan of the scales, made adjustments and then poured the contents into a cone bag or later a square paper bag, was magical.

Just a little of the range were: Black Jacks, Fruit Salads, licquorice root, Flying Saucers, Hubba Bubba bubble gum, Little Imps, Cherry Lips, Love Hearts, Victory V Lozenges, aniseed balls, Sports Mixture, sweet cigarettes, Camel brand chocolate cigarettes, gob stoppers, sherbet dips, Lucky Bags. Riley's Chocolate Toffee Rolls, Refreshers, parma violets, bananas, shrimps, sherbert fountains, walnut whips, cinder toffee, treacle toffee lollies in silver tart trays, toffee apples, Smith's crisps with little blue twisted bags of salt, Sunpat raisins, pear drops, lemon drops, acid drops, cough candy, mint humbugs, rock, sherbet lemons, dolly mixtures, allsorts and jelly babies. I am sure that I have probably missed out your favourites.

You left the shop with your little bag and all was right with the world. Apparently, there was ether and chloroform in the Victory V lozenges and there was an enforced change of recipe and they were never the same again. For those who are uninitiated, liquorice root was the actual root of a plant. It was a yellow colour and when chewed it gave off a strong liquorice taste mixed with woody splinters. It was definitely an acquired taste and the woody residue had to be spat into the bins.

My christening April 1955

The shop also sold comics and there were Superhero ones from the USA. I enjoyed the stories, but what always fascinated me were the adverts. I remember X-Ray glasses, sea monkeys. Apparently sea monkeys were some sort of brine shrimp that were in suspended animation when dried, but came back to life when poured into a jar of water. Of course the fact that we couldn't buy what American children could, made them even more desirable. When you were really flush you may have left the shop with lollies and a comic.

If for some reason the shop was closed, there were a couple of coin operated dispensing machines. One would dispense mint chewing gum in packets and another bubble gum balls. You put your penny in, waited for it to drop, turned the handle and listened for the gum to drop. If you were really lucky, you might find two when you opened the door to the drawer. On those days, your state of bliss knew no boundaries.

As I have said before, I was in Mr. Kelly's Year 4 class and I am sure the class size was about forty. He was a middle-aged man, though all teachers seemed ancient to me. He wasn't particularly tall. I seem to remember Mr. Woods, the deputy, being tall though. Mr Kelly had yellow stains on the fingers of his right hand. I remember him being asked whether it was from smoking and he denied this. He claimed it was from cutting apples at lunch time. We were naïve then, but I don't think any of us fell for that. I was told that his white hair was the result of a war injury. During WWII, he was recovering in hospital and a nurse thought he was an old man as his hair had turned white overnight from the shock. His class was very orderly and we sat in pairs in rows, all facing the front in a room with bare wooden floorboards and large windows down one side. The top windows could be opened only by using the long window pole that hooked onto a ring and allowed them to be pulled forward, hinged from the bottom, to let in air. Thick central heating pipes ran around the wall under the windows. Occasionally he would be frustrated and he could certainly shout!

SMOG, FOG AND BUSES

In the early sixties in Leeds, children either walked to and from school, or they caught a bus. There was none of the over-indulged, fear-driven need for mummy to escort you to the door of the classroom in a vehicle built to withstand a nuclear attack and the size of a tank. No one demanded half an hour of the teacher's time, whilst everyone else waited, ensuring that their needs were being met. There was no cross-examination at the end of the day to check that no one had been mean to you. (You see the effect a lifetime in education has had on me!) Not at all! In fact, on my first day at Harehills my mother did escort me to the school gates, the only time ever, I might add, and I upset her as she gazed through the bars of the fence by saying, 'Would you please go away!' She did, probably with a broken heart, and I never looked back and loved my time there.

I was used to using buses. My first school was Stainbeck Preparatory School and I started there at four years old. I used to travel to and from school on two buses with my elder brother, and when he left when I was six I used to travel on my own. Nowadays, my mother would probably be seen as wildly negligent, but at the time I don't think it was anything out of the ordinary. We would catch a bus from Arlington Road/Easterly Road junction and change at Harehills and travel through Chapel Allerton down to Stainbeck Lane. I remember one very cold frosty morning, passing a milk float, an electric one that the driver walked in front of with a control handle. It had toppled over on the ice on a steep side road towards Chapel Allerton Hospital and a white river of milk was pouring down the street. At the time, I wondered if the milkman would have lost his job as a result.

Anyway, I usually walked to Harehills and saved the bus fare, but I would catch the bus home normally as it was all uphill and a bit of a slog. Double-decker buses in those days had a driver in a separate cab at the front and a conductor, who took your money, gave you a ticket and told you off if you misbehaved or failed to stand to give up your seat to a lady or an elderly person. I think the fare was a penny and the large heavy coins were a wonderful feel: tactile, solid and usually well-worn. I loved the ticket machine. Coins were stored in special storage tubes on a leather belt and with a quick flick of the thumb from the conductor, change would appear in his or her hand. Another flick of the thumb and the correct ticket was dispensed and there was a ripping sound as it was separated from the roll of tickets. If you were lucky, the tickets would run out and the conductor would open the machine and fit a new roll of tickets. It was quite a to-do and appealed to my senses. Another feature I was fascinated by was the bell buttons. There were round white affairs, with 'Push Once' printed on them and there was a bright red button in the middle. As a small lad they were well above my reach and, in fact, only the conductor could use them. It is probably something Freudian, but I really wanted to push them. Some conductors would give a jaunty double push to tell the driver to set off. They were replaced on more modern buses with a strip, which reminded me of a hose pipe that you could push from anywhere along the aisle.

Most conductors, I remember, seemed to enjoy the job. The young men liked to hang on the pole at the open end of the bus, lean out, show off their skill and impress young ladies or easily-influenced boys. They were masters of their steed: hats perched on, often quite long hair. In many ways they appeared a poor man's Waltzer attendant from the fairground with their daring dos on the pole, their debonair panache as they sold tickets to teenage girls and swaggered up the aisles. No matter how bumpy the ride, they were balanced, in control and then disappeared up the stairs to the top deck like dancers.

The upstairs of the buses were often smoke-filled and if you went up you often felt sick before too long, as the deck swayed alarmingly. The upstairs had great views, particularly from the front seats and there was a sign that said, 'Spitting is Forbidden', but occasionally old men could be heard clearing their throats. Oh, how times have changed!

Grandma, Dad, Mum, Aunty Joan, Uncle Ernest Sabot the dog and probably Aunty Maud.

The bus ride from Harehills up Easterly Road was only short and I knew the trip like the back of my hand, but on one afternoon the fog was in. Fog in those days was something else. It really was fog, or smog and the mist would be a dark green, due to the heavy smoke from all the coal fires. Before the introduction of smokeless coal, followed shortly by the disappearance of domestic fires, smoke was ever-present. I grew up thinking that the main buildings in Leeds were made of black stone. The Town Hall was this black, overpowering, serious building, until they started to sand-blast the city buildings in the 1960s. It was quite a revelation to see these stone buildings appear in their naked glory as yellow/white, gleaming and very impressive monuments to wealth and power of Northern England. But on this specific day, the fog was dense and olive green. I can still taste the air, chemical filled and bitter. It wasn't just a cosmetic danger. Bronchial disease would kill about 30,000 people each year in London alone.

I waited outside school at the bus stop in the gloom. The sound was changed by the air thickness and pale orbs of light could barely be seen from the street lights. Of course, being winter in England meant it was dark when we left school and cars crawled past as we waited for the bus. You had to be careful to get on the right bus as the numbers on the front could barely be seen, even when they stopped in front of you. A wrong choice and you could end up at Oakwood and I did make this mistake at least once. My bus arrived and I got on and sat on the sideways-facing bench seats near the open section as it allowed some view outside. Further in, all the windows were steamed up and you had no idea where you were. The bus crawled along Roundhay Road and the shops aided me in telling where I was, but as we slowly turned at the roundabout by the Clock Cinema and headed up the hill, all knowledge of where I was vanished. The world disappeared completely and the swirling miasma transformed the vista into a nightmare of uncertainty. It was so dense you truly could see nothing and I have always had perfect eyesight. I began to panic and decided I must be near my stop and the conductor rang the bell and the bus came to a halt and I stepped down into darkness and confusion. The air was damp and heavy, but as I watched the bus drive off I realised I was not at my stop. I was still on the hill so I worked out I must have got off too soon. I almost panicked, but I knew if I just headed up the hill I would eventually reach a little ginnel that led through our estate to my house, and so I did. Finally, I got my bearings and reached the ginnel and made my way home, a little shaken by the experience.

As I got older, I became bolder with the bus journey and I developed the skill of hanging off the bar well before the bus arrived at the stop. The ability to jump off the bus whilst it was slowing down and hit the ground running was what was craved and, apart from a couple of embarrassing miscalculations, I honed the skill to perfection. The joys of youth!

SUNKEN SHIPS AND BURIED TREASURE!

Well do I remember one warm, sunny afternoon in Leeds when my grandma came to our house and took my younger brother and me for an outing to Roundhay Park. I don't think that my elder brother was with us on this occasion, but I am sure he will let me know if I am wrong. The walk to Roundhay was quite a long one. We had to go through Gipton Woods to Oakwood and then across the vast sports pitches of the Soldiers' Fields to the Park itself. The park was and still is a most beautiful area. It was originally the grounds of a large stately home, now just called the Mansion. The park had sports fields and two lakes: one large, the Big Lake as we called it, (Waterloo Lake); and the other smaller, the Little Lake, (Upper Lake). Both had boats for hire: the Big Lake, rowing boats; and the Little Lake, small wooden paddle boats, which you powered with handles.

Now as I have explained before, my grandma was a short plump lady, who struggled to walk long distances, but she was game and we trailed along with her. We arrived at the Little Lake and she paid the ticket for a boat. The attendant pulled one to the side with a long boat hook and my brother got in. The paddle boats were brightly painted and would hold three children or a couple of adults. The water in the Little Lake was only shallow and we used to use fishing nets to catch minnows to keep in a jar, but it was deep enough to cause difficulty if you fell in. Both of the lakes were man-made and part of the landscaping of the grounds, but over time the bottom had accumulated a lot of sediment and rotting plant matter and was definitely not something you would want to paddle around in.

The paddle boats were something that my brothers and I had used many times and we were quite capable of being let loose alone, but on this occasion, maybe because of the heat, Grandma decided to have a go. She asked the man and he said it would be alright. My younger brother got in and the man held the boat with his hook whilst my grandma took her turn. It was quite a step down and she had to hitch up her dress, revealing quite a bit of chubby pink leg and maybe it was this that distracted the man. She didn't position her foot in the centre of the boat and as she lowered her weight, the boat rolled to the side and water started filling it. My younger brother feared for his life and scrambled to try and get out. The boatman panicked and pulled my grandma to safety and I just stood there watching in amazement. My brother jumped for the wall of the lake and scrambled ashore, but in the process lost one of his sandals and it fell back into the water and no amount of searching with the boat hook could find it.

No one was injured physically, but my grandma's pride definitely took a beating and she was also worried about the repercussions of returning to our mother to explain what had happened. She had nearly fallen in and lost her handbag, but the boatman had discovered strength he did not know he possessed. She led my brother by the hand to the ice cream van that was nearby and we were bought 99's (ice cream in a cone with a chocolate Flake) to keep us quiet and happy, whilst she decided on a plan of action. The weather wasn't a problem and the walk to Oakwood village could all be done on soft grass. She told my brother that she would buy him a new pair of sandals at the shops on the way home.

We headed back home with ice creams in hand, leaving a relieved boatman helping other paying customers. We made the slower journey to Oakwood and the sandals were replaced. I seem to remember the leather expensive sandals were substituted with a plastic pair. Looking back, I can only assume my grandma was devastated and worried about the repercussions and that my mother would think she wasn't safe to be let loose with her children. I know money was tight, so the additional cost would have been an issue for her. I believe, in the end, my mother was just relieved that we were all alright, but I am not sure what my father's reaction was. For my brother and me, we just added it to the rich tapestry of growing up experiences.

On many other occasions when we were at my Grandma's house we were allowed the button box. This was a biscuit tin filled with a vast range of buttons. I am not sure if they were cast-offs that my Grandad brought home from tailoring, or just what had been removed from old clothes, saved in case of some possible need in the future. I loved the button tin. It was magical. Not only did it have buttons of all shapes and sizes, but it also had jewels. Well, maybe not real ones, but glass jewelled buttons, some large and brightly coloured. They shimmered in the light as their prismatic shapes caught the sun and my imagination. Those buttons were treasure. A pirate's hoard from some ne'er-do-well buccaneer and they were mine, all mine! I lifted handfuls and let them fall back through my fingers and the touch and sound took me even further from reality. I could play for hours with the buttons, in front of the fire and I was lost in ecstatic dreams and visions. The coal and the flames led me to a volcanic island and there I discovered the hoard. I can still feel their touch and their weight. What more could a young boy want? Well, maybe a real treasure hunt, but that will have to wait for another time.

CRAFT, ART AND COUNTRY DANCING

I am approaching the end of my memories of Harehills C. P. School, but there are still some that you might have shared. One of these is the art and craft lessons that we had. I think I am remembering Mr. Kelly's class, but it could have been younger years that have merged. One thing I remember we did every Easter time, was to make wool pompoms. Two circles of card were cut and a smaller circle was cut out of the centre of each. The two card circles were placed together and wool, at this time of year, yellow wool was wound around the card. This must have been heaven for the teachers as it took hours to wind sufficient wool around, producing a woollen doughnut at the end. At this point the teacher took over and cut around the edge of the doughnut and then tied a tight loop between the card circles. When the wool was then fluffed out it produced a pompom. Each of us then produced a slightly smaller pompom and the two finished balls were fixed together and then a felt beak and two eyes were added to produce an Easter chick.

Each Christmas, I seem to remember having to collect holly to bring to school. The holly was cut into smaller pieces and we had a shallow dish into which the holly, pine cones and a candle were placed, before plaster of Paris was poured in and allowed to set. When this was set, the tray was removed. Some glitter and maybe spray paint, gold or silver was sprayed on the holly and cones before fixing and then a ribbon was tied around the edge. At the end of the Christmas term, I remember carefully carrying the candle set home for my mum. I have often wondered how many houses were set alight by similar decorations produced at schools.

Another craft activity was simple embroidery on binka, the material with holes to guide young hands. Cross-stitching and other techniques were used to produce bookmarks, or maybe a place mat. Names would be embroidered on them and it kept children busy for hours and the teachers occupied re-threading needles, bodkins and undoing mistakes. I also remember learning how to do simple knitting. The class were set the task of knitting squares of basic stitches and these were joined up to make a blanket. I seem to remember it was for some charity such as Oxfam and it was presented in assembly. The other type of knitting that we learnt was French knitting. This meant we had to bring in wooden cotton reels. I think four small nails were hammered into the top and you wound wool in a certain way and then unhooked it and it formed a sausage of wool through the hole in the reel. Eventually it was removed and sewn into a round disk of knitted wool, which could be used as a place mat.

These experiences must have been before being in Mr. Kelly's class as I can't think he was into needlework. I specifically do remember making matchbox tricks that involved a loop of brown gummed tape. I can still remember the strong specific taste of the glue on the tape. The trick was that you opened the box, put a penny in it, or similar coin, and then shut the box. You would say a magic word and open the box and the coin would disappear. This amazing trick was very simple and a loop of brown tape would hide the coin if the box was opened from the other end and it could reappear, by simply opening it from the original end. We also made a cardboard wallet with a cover of marbled ink. I loved the marbling as it produced such a wonderful swirl of colours as the inks were floated on water and the paper laid on top. The wallet was constructed with diagonal ribbons that crossed the covers and similar to the matchbox trick, a note placed in the wallet could be made to vanish when the wallet was opened and closed. The trick was in the way you opened and closed the wallet. One way the note was hidden behind the cover and the other way it was at the front.

Mr. Kelly's magic tricks must have impressed me, as I did some tricks in a talent show at the end of one term. I just used some tricks from a box of magic tricks I had for a birthday and performed in front of the school. I made coins disappear in a hanky and could tell what card someone chose from a pack. It can't have been too exciting for the audience that were a long way off. Other performers were dancers, musical turns and even some children miming to a song.

We did once have a craft fair and we could enter a whole range of things. I was at a loss what to do, but with help from my mum and dad we decided on a desert scene. A square terracotta pot was bought with a few cacti. A small mirror was placed amongst the cacti and then fine white sand poured over the potting compost. The mirror produced a lake and it made a decent desert scene. I then added some tiny Airfix Bedouin figures and tiny camels to finish the scene. I remember carefully carrying it into school and it was put on display with other entries. There were different categories and I remember getting a star or something similar for mine and I proudly took it home where it went on display in the front room window, where it lasted for a long time..

Now one vivid memory I do have is country dancing. Again, I don't think Mr. Kelly was the teacher who took this. We were paired up, boy/girl in two long lines or sometimes in a circle and we were taught the basic steps. We must have challenged the patience of the teacher as most of us boys were either rhythmically or otherwise challenged. Eventually, with a lot of counting, one, two, three, four, over and over again, we managed the basics and some sort of order appeared and something resembling a dance was produced. I don't remember if we ever danced at the May dance in Roundhay Park, or whether we just went along to watch those accomplished performers who had got beyond the most simple of dances. I did enjoy it though and maybe it was the holding of a girl's hand as we danced that gave it added excitement. Certainly, hormones were happening in the final year and there was a lot of interest in birthday parties and who was invited. Post Man's Knock was as far as it ever got, but it was the start of the change that truly set in in high school. I could see why there was a girls' and a boys' school at Roundhay, but the thorny holly hedge proved little barrier for the horny teenagers we were to become.

My time at Harehills was a golden time in my life. We were learning, loving learning, full of optimism in a world that was changing so rapidly after the Second World War. Science was going to be the saviour of our bright new world and in many ways it has been. It was a time of improvement for the world and the people who inhabited the planet and we saw such change. Unfortunately, children are presented with doom and gloom scenarios now at school, even though great strides have been made in health, pollution, energy production and standard of living. In the early sixties, there were major outbreaks of diseases such as polio, measles, mumps, rubella, rickets, smallpox, bronchitis and many others. At Christmas, the television stations would visit hospitals and we would see people in iron lungs and others less fortunate. We don't see that now very often as many diseases are almost eradicated from our lives. We were some of the first to be inoculated for childhood diseases and saw real benefits.

TRIPS TO THE CINEMA

As a child, one of the highlights was a trip to the cinema. My earliest memories are of going to the cinema with my grandmother at The Dominion in Chapel Allerton. There were two types of cinema visits, depending on who took me and my brothers. If it was my mum or my grandmother, then it was normally cartoons or musicals, but if it was my father it was usually cowboys or adventure films.

It wasn't a long walk to the Dominion in Chapel Allerton, but at a young age it seemed a long way, particularly after one of grandma's extremely filling dinners. My grandmother was a short, stout lady and walking always seemed to make her out of breath. The cinema dominated the corner opposite the primary school towards the next parade of shops and it was quite a majestic building. I am unsure as to whether the first time was Dumbo or Fantasia, but certainly they are my first memories. They were not new films even in those days, but still firm favourites with children and adults. On later occasions we went to see new releases before the cinema closed in 1967. Mary Poppins (1964) and the Sound of Music (1965) were two of the films we saw there. It was a real treat and I don't know how much it cost her, but I know she never had a lot of spare money. No visit to the cinema would have been complete without either a Kia-ora orange drink in a plastic beaker with a foil top, an ice-cream tub with a small wooden spoon, or Butterkist popcorn. I can still taste the creamy flavour, mixed with the wooden taste of the spoon. It was only ever one of the three. The treat was normally bought during the intermission, halfway through the film, or between the B-movie and the main film. A lady with a tray would march down the aisle and stand at the front whilst a queue of eager children, or parents would form. The sizes of the drinks and tubs were tiny compared to what people would expect nowadays.

When we entered the cinema we entered a world of wonder. There were people in uniforms and tickets were bought at the foyer ticket booth. Clasping the tickets, we went up the stairs, had them torn in half by the man or lady on guard and headed through double doors with round windows into a strange, vast space with row upon row of seats. This was short trouser time and in fact it was shorts until the second year of Roundhay School. We would find a seat, not too far back, not too near the front, shuffle along to try and get to the middle and then would sit. This wasn't easy when you were little, as the seats had to be pushed down before you could climb onto them. When you were sitting, the pile of the seat fabric would push into your legs and they could go a little dead if it was a long film or a double bill. Grandma would normally sit between my brother and me. I am not sure if this was so she could control us better, or to stop us interacting and misbehaving.

After a long wait and the influx of patrons, the lights would dim a little and there would be twenty minutes of adverts. I am not sure if Pearl and Dean were advertising when I was very little, but they were when I got older. I've just checked this and they started in 1953, so it would have been them. These were rather boring, but the trailers that followed showed films that would be on soon and they were much more interesting. Finally, the lights would drop down to almost pitch black and the film would start. Sometimes, there was a round of applause, if there was a large young audience, and then we were captivated by a world of wonder and colour. Not all films were in colour, but the Disney ones were. I remember well 101 Dalmatians and the nightmares I had for years after. Cruella De Vil scared the life out of me, but even worse was the Disney film, Darby O'Gill and the Little People. The Banshee arriving with the ghostly carriage still haunts me to this day. I am not sure that storytellers in the 1940s, 50s and 60s had the same concern for the emotional welfare of children that they do today. Or was it just me being a sensitive soul?

Regardless of a couple of trauma-inducing parts of the films, my experience was mainly joyous and grandma seemed to enjoy them. Afterwards, we would wearily make our way back to her house in Regent Terrace and even more food. The Dominion closed and our trips then would be to The Clock Cinema. As we were older, my brother and I would sometimes go to the Saturday Matinee. This was a thrill for a number of reasons. The first was because we went on our own and the second was because it was a bit of a wild experience. The matinee would start with the rigid control of the male usher who would leave us in no doubt that any misbehaving would be very severely dealt with and this started with the orderly queuing to pay for the tickets. There were hordes of excited children of quite a range of ages and they chatted frenetically and tended to push from behind. Woe betide anyone who was caught! Their afternoon excitement would end before it even started and the usher had a memory like an elephant and he would catch those foolish enough to try and enter again. A physical clip on the ear was not totally out of the question. Once we had passed the first test and got our tickets we entered the cinema proper.

The Clock was bigger than The Dominion and grander. It looked much more like a theatre than a cinema and it was resplendent, with layers of curtaining that were raised and pulled apart to reveal the screen. I believe there was even an organ that could rise up in front, but maybe that is just wishful thinking. The noise in the cinema filled with hundreds of children was deafening and the excitement was even greater if you were on the upper level. Attendants patrolled, torches in hand, and there was no hesitation in evicting anyone who upset them in any way. Trips to the toilets were scrutinised to ensure that rogue children weren't allowed admission through the fire exit. We did try it a few times as we got older, but the attendants would often check the tickets of those returning from the toilets. It must have come as a great relief when the show started. There were no films of any great merit. Silent movies would be mixed with a range of cowboy films, often The Lone Ranger. Laurel and Hardy were still on the go and I am sure that I remember a very early silent movie of Batman. I know there was a 1926 film, The Bat, which was an inspiration for Batman, but I am sure I remember Batman climbing on old cars in chases. What I do remember well was that the films always seemed to snap or melt during the most exciting parts. Great cries of anguish would erupt from the audience, the lights would come on with a slide telling us that the performance would resume as soon as possible. The attendants went into action. An example would be made of a group and an eviction occurred and this had a calming effect on the remainder.

After what seemed like a lifetime, the film would have been spliced and off we went again. The lights dimmed and applause resounded around the cinema. Eventually, the show ended and tired, but still excited droves of kids left through the exits and I am sure that some of the attendants would have heaved a sigh of relief, some needing a stiff drink. In winter, dusk would be setting in and we would trudge up the hill of Upland Road to our house in Gipton Wood Crescent.

We did go to the cinema with my mum or my dad, but never together. I believe it was used to give them a bit of time on their own.

PLAYGROUND ADVENTURES

One of the major changes from the childhood I experienced and that my grandchildren have is that of playgrounds. Modern playgrounds are colourful, well-built, architecturally designed and above all safe, whereas ours were sparse, dull-coloured, barren areas, but more than anything were exciting and dangerous.

Who can forget the slides that towered over the parks? Bare metal, steep-angled and the climb up the metal rungs was enough to raise the heart rate and provide a wide view as we towered above the surrounding area. The views alone were worth the danger. They did offer two alternatives for children: the lower slides that were intended for younger children, but these were still higher than many modern slides, and the big slide, and these were, or at least appeared to be in my memory, towering structures. With a nod to safety, the tops were sometimes caged in and a small platform was where you awaited your turn to shoot down the highly polished steel slide at breakneck speeds. The edges of the slide were low and offered little room for error and the base was often a mixture of tarmac, concrete, mud and gravel. The angle of incline was very steep and with an addition shove, or swing off the cage, extra momentum propelled you at death defying speeds, or so it seemed. When reaching the bottom, the slide levelled off and the thin metal allowed legs to dangle over the sides to brake the impetus and enable a safe stop. That, at least, was the intent, but as we became older the sensible use was not exciting enough and variations were created to increase the risk, the danger and thus the pleasure. Head first was an obvious adaptation and on a good slide it could result in flying off the end and getting a faceful of gravel and grazes, cut knees and other scars that were worn as a badge of valour. Only the youngest children were supervised and as we got older our parents probably felt that what they didn't see us do was better for their nerves.

My knees still bear witness to minor accidents, but somehow we all seemed to survive fairly intact. I now wonder if the casualty departments at St James' Hospital or the Infirmary may have told a different tale.

Each slide had its own personality and characteristics. Some were slower, some steeper, some wider and my favourite, I think, was at Potternewton Park. I may be wrong there, but the one I am picturing was a partially green painted structure that allowed almost supersonic speed for what seemed to last for a long time.

If you survived, or tired of the slides, there were other challenges. The roundabouts were fantastic fun. If there were families using them with little children then they were sedate frames that consisted of a circular wooden base on a metal frame and the circle was divided by four metal rails that allowed you to hold on whilst the whole structure revolved around a central column of steel. The base was about five or six inches above the playground surface. Young children would hang onto the handrails and parents would slowly push the roundabout, making sure the child was secure and safe. Slightly bigger children would jump on and off in the manner that the designers probably intended.

When the roundabout was free of youngsters and adults then we made full use in an entirely different manner. Speed was of the essence. You would hold on to the rail and run, pushing the roundabout as fast as you could, and we really could get up a speed. At maximum velocity and just before you were dragged off your feet, you jumped onto the revolving platform and hung on for dear life. The centrifugal force was trying to throw you off, but you clung on, feeling the wind on your face and through your hair, laughing and challenging the world to do its worst as you were up to it. Such is the esprit of youth. To make it more interesting you would hang backwards and the challenge was to get as low to the ground as possible. The real art was to have the back of your head just above the ground and you hoped there weren't any lumps as your hair brushed the gravel. Eventually, exhaustion, friction and nausea would put an end to the ride. Who can forget the dizziness of the spinning world and the inability to maintain your stance? We would stagger around like drunkards until our heads cleared.

Accidents did happen, but not often and I never saw any major ones. I did see children lose their footing as they ran pushing the roundabout as fast as possible and get dragged along before letting go. The injuries tended to be very nasty, deep grazes that hurt and took a long time to heal. The scabs on your legs would pull as they became hard and started to weep. Even worse was when they began to itch as they healed and finally dropped off or were scratched off. Germolene seemed to heal everything and I can still smell its distinct aroma.

The other challenge of the roundabout was the ability to jump on and off whilst it was going. To impress everyone else around, this meant choosing maximum speed as the opportunity to demonstrate one's skill. Timing had to be just right and you had to hit the ground running or catastrophe would occur. Planting yourself face first onto a round surface would be bad enough and extremely painful, but much more painful was making a fool of yourself in front of others and losing face, sometimes quite literally. Many a time I witnessed such falls from grace as a cool (don't think we used the term 'cool' then) youth lost all credibility with a disastrous dismount. The most dangerous and highest status trick was to jump onto a speedily revolving roundabout, avoiding the bar and landing and staying on your feet. Only the foolhardy would attempt this and I suppose that Darwin would say it was survival of the fittest as many came a cropper.

There was no limit to our creativity when riding the roundabouts. You could hang upside down on the bars whilst riding, lie upon the top of the bar, sit on the central hub, or the base, the variations were endless. You could sit and read the Beano or Topper, but that tended to make you quite sick after a while.

The playgrounds may have lacked creative designs, but a child's imagination could make them wonderlands. There was other equipment and the wooden see-saw was a must. Young children would be carefully held on by adoring parents but as we got bigger we wanted fun and that meant bouncing up and down with real force. I can still feel the shock of the wood hitting the concrete and the shuddering vibration passing up your spine as you pushed up as hard as you could to inflict a similar punishment on the back of the child opposite. If you were on your own you could stand on the top and, legs on either side of the pivot, move the plank up and down. Again we developed the knack of jumping off the see-saw whilst it was in motion. The danger here was you had to get clear, otherwise the plank of solid timber could strike you. I remember being struck under the chin and it must have been similar to a good uppercut from a heavyweight boxer.

Another piece of equipment that was disappearing even then, was something I have been informed was called a Witch's Hat. There was a tall central pole of solid steel that was probably three or four yards standing above the ground and supported on it was a cone shape metal frame that was pivoted at the top. Much like the roundabout, it could be pushed to revolve, but it had the added bonus of also moving up and down as it balanced. The frame was about two or three feet off ground level to allow for the up and down movement and it really was for bigger children as the youngsters couldn't climb on by themselves. All the dangers of the roundabout and other equipment seemed to be collected onto the one set of apparatus as it spun and dipped and rose. I guess it must have had problems as they were being removed over time.

Of course, the compulsory swings were in every playground. There were the milk-crate designed ones for little children where they sat in a wooden frame and the legs had to be slipped in so they were secure. As you got a bit bigger the problem was getting out and it required adult help to pull you out whilst the frame dangled off your legs. The swings for the oldies were basically a wooden board held by chains. There was a real joy in swinging when little, as your parents pushed you and would sing songs like 'See-Saw Margery Daw', but swinging solo required technique to get going. You rocked your body to build up momentum and height. Teenage years saw us become immortal, or so we thought, and danger added to the developing emotions. Rising above the ordinary, both literally and figuratively, was important and the swing offered both. The one who could reach the highest had more kudos than the others. I have seen people reach almost the vertical, where gravity overcomes centrifugal force (I know science has replaced centrifugal force, but that was what we believed at the time) and the swinger fell vertically down and the fall was broken by the chains and there was a sharp bounce.

Nevertheless' there was a great joy in swinging high and staring down onto a world with a totally different perspective. There was an intense feeling of being alive and the teenage years saw the extremes of emotions: euphoria and misery went up and down like the see-saw and swings of the playground. We didn't care that the equipment was dangerous and misused. Life was like that. We could experience danger and either learn to manage it or suffer the consequences. Today we have taken much of that experience away. The modern child no longer faces any dangers and therefore does not develop the skills to know their limitations and the potential consequences, until they are seventeen and we allow them to take control of a car. Is it any wonder they have so many accidents? Maybe our dangerous playgrounds made us safer in the long run. All I really know is that we had such great times!

HORACE, HECTOR AND PENNY.

In a previous tale I mentioned the rabbit we looked after when the owners were on holiday and that got me thinking about some of the pets that we kept whilst we lived at Lawrence Avenue and Gipton Wood Crescent. Families, such as ours, kept a variety of pets and since then public attitudes and feelings have changed. This is one area that I feel the world, at least in the Western world, has changed for the better.

In my childhood in the 1950s and 60s, it was not unusual for tortoises to be kept as pets, a practice that has now almost disappeared. Clearly, tortoises were not native to the cold climates of England and whilst they seemed quite happy to live in the garden, eating dandelions and lettuce, they were challenged during the colder months of the year. Blue Peter, on television, used to keep a tortoise and they wrote its name on its shell with white paint and it would appear as a regular until it was autumn and then they would have a big session on how to care for one over winter. The original one on Blue Peter was called Fred and it lived from 1963 to 79. This seems a fair age, but in reality, the Mediterranean tortoise should live to about 90 and many can go beyond this age. In time it was recognised that the Blue Peter one wasn't a boy at all and they added an 'A' and Fred became Freda.

Winter meant putting them in a box filled with straw and placing them in the loft of the house, where it was expected that they would hibernate until spring. We had three tortoises when we were still in Lawrence Avenue and they were lovely creatures that seemed content to do little but eat. We had Hector, Horace and a little one that we called Penny. They were slow moving, but they could still get around the garden if you didn't watch out for them. The hard, shiny shells were beautiful and they couldn't have been very old. Penny was so small it must have been very young. It was bought from a pet shop, probably the one at Harehills, next to the café across from Varley's toy shop. Pet shops were very different from today. It was not seen as cruel to buy pets and I think the change in attitude to the one we have nowadays is a major improvement. Dogs, rabbits, kittens and even exotic pets could be bought with little fuss. We decided we wanted a tortoise and so we just went and bought one. There was no check on whether you knew how to look after them.

It is often thought a good thing for children to have pets in their lives, but I am not so sure. My experience has been that children very quickly tire of them once the initial enthusiasm has waned and it is left to the adults to deal with the care, the cleaning and the ensuring they come to no harm. The more exotic pets such as tortoises were not bred in the UK. They were imported from their natural habitat of Greece. Apparently boatloads of tortoises, piled up in baskets, arrived on the docks and then were transported to pet shops. The local fauna numbers must have been devastated, but we didn't know and I am not sure we would have cared in the way we would today.

The first tortoise, Horace, arrived at our house in summer and it was kept in a box inside the house with water and food and when we could we would take it into the garden where it seemed very happy to roam and would munch on the few flowers there were. A little pen of chicken-wire was set up so it could roam safely, after it had made a mad dash to escape the garden and search for more interesting pastures in the neighbouring garden. My dad also made it a small wooden house where it would be safe from cats etc. I was fascinated by the way it could disappear into its shell and then reappear when tempted by a tasty piece of greenery. The small plates on its legs and neck made it a living dinosaur as far as I was concerned and there were no boys who didn't love dinosaurs.

Blue Peter would indicate the time for preparing for hibernation and we would get it ready by collecting a stout box, straw and newspaper. The poor thing was placed in the box and it must have wondered what was happening. It was then taken into the loft by my dad and left to its own devices for the winter. Now this seems fine in theory and in the Blue Peter world where, 'Here is one I prepared earlier', ensured they never failed. Viewers would not have known whether Freda (Fred) was the same as the one seen from previous year. (Am I being cynical?) Well, theirs seemed to survive for quite a long time, but certainly not as long as it would have done in the wild in its natural habitat, but ours managed a year or two before one year we all forgot poor Horace. It was well into spring when we remembered and, of course, the poor thing had come out of hibernation and died, probably of thirst. This must have happened all around the UK. It would only take a mild spell and they would come out of hibernation and unless the families checked they would have met the same fate as ours. After three attempts to care for the wonderfully delightful creatures, we finally called it a day. We would never willingly have hurt any of our pets, but ignorance at the time meant that animals suffered at the hands of well-meaning families.

The lesson my brothers and I took from the pets we had, and other children do, is that life has an end. The upset one feels at the loss of a pet is quite genuine and even as an adult, heart-breaking. At various times and in both our houses animals were laid to rest in the flowerbeds and sometimes marked with a little cross and a few words of sadness.

THE LITTLE WOODS AND GIPTON WOOD.

My family moved from Lawrence Avenue to Gipton Wood Crescent at a time when my brothers and I had reached an age where playing out was what you did. When not at school, you were expected to move out of the house and occupy yourselves in a number of ways. One, as I have spoken about in the past, was to visit my grandma's in Chapel Allerton; others were to play in the garden, the street or in our case either what we called the Little Woods (Fairy Woods) or Gipton Wood itself, which we thought of as the Big Woods.

The Little Woods was an area between the houses that could be accessed through two narrow ginnels, (alleys). It had a few trees and a lot of rough grass area and a mound that we thought of as a bomb site, with a crater in the middle. It had clearly been there a long time as large trees had grown around and in it. I can not think why this large area was left and nowadays such architectural planning would be seen as a waste, but it provided a great playground for children in the area. We could ride our bikes safely and tracks and jumps crisscrossed the dip and it was great fun. We played soccer and cricket on a rough bare patch that challenged the very best batsman to predict the bounce, but we didn't care. In summer the grass would grow tall and it was a perfect place to hide and seek. We would crawl for hours through the grass, defying anyone to spot us, and would build dens. It was only when we returned home at night we realised how itchy we were from all the grass cuts. The Little Woods was an oasis of peace amongst the semi-detached suburbia that surrounded it. I can't recall ever seeing adults and no one took dogs for a walk there. In those times taking a dog for a walk usually meant opening the door and letting it out on its own. No one worried and no one collected dog poo!

As children, we could stay out as long as we wanted and only returned for meals or in the evening when it was time for bed. We weren't unusual in this and we enjoyed a freedom that children nowadays would envy. Looking back, there must have been dangers, but there wasn't the publicity that we now experience. We even played in the Little Woods at night and we took torches to play Wide Games with searchlights as we sneaked up to the base. Luckily, there weren't dangerous creatures in Leeds and I am not sure I would want to play the same games here in Australia, where there is a plethora of things to sting or bite lurking in the undergrowth.

On more adventurous days we would go to Gipton Wood. Now for those who don't know this part of Leeds, Gipton Wood is a sizeable woodland of oaks, sycamores, beech trees and others. The mixed woodland is full of bluebells and when they are out, the ground is a lavender carpet that is quite breathtaking. The canopy is very dense and parts of the woods are very dark and, at the time, were not well-travelled. As a child, I could play most of the day at the north eastern part and not see other people all day. The woods were bequeathed to the City for recreational use and together with Gledhow Valley and Roundhay Park form a wonderful green corridor in this part of the city. There were two main pathways and these ran from the houses where we lived through to either Oakwood village, or cut down the hill to Roundhay Road near the Gipton pub. There were steps that led down to the old tram lines and I remember well my brother Andrew riding his bike down them, against all common sense, and him going head over heels over the top of the handlebars. This I must say was only one of a number of accidents he had as a child and it really is a miracle that he grew to adulthood. Another incident involved him cycling adjacent to me down Gipton Wood Crescent, towards the woods and he was so engrossed in the conversation that he didn't notice the lorry, (truck), parked at the side of the road and despite my warnings he just rode straight into the back of it. Another good one was sledging on the frame of a rocking donkey and nearly killing himself, but that will have to wait for another time.

The woods were really in three sections: there was the flat north eastern section, the sloping central area that fell sharply to Roundhay Road and the very steep small valley at the southern boundary, that had a small stream flowing from a spring. Each section offered different adventures to us when we played. In winter the central slope provided a sledge run when there was snow, but was crossed by a pathway and had a single electric light in a lantern that seemed to have come out of The Lion, The Witch and The Wardrobe. At night it was the only source of light in the wood and it cast a cone of light amongst the pitch black of the woods. This caused me some scary moments as a teenager, when I would walk home through the woods late at night. I was never sure if it was my mood or the mood of the woods, but sometimes I walked through and never had any concerns about safety, but at other times it was very scary and I would often end up running to get out. You would think that the pool of light would help, but actually it was worse, as when you entered the light everything outside was black. Ten people could have been standing there watching you and you would have had no idea. I guess it was all in my mind as I never had any incidents and I got so used to it that I knew where to lift my feet as roots crossed the pathway, ready to trip the unwary.

I had a lot of fun in the quieter, more deserted north eastern section. I have only recently found out that this section holds the remains of a Bronze Age camp. The shallow trenches that provided good hiding spots for hide a seek were part of the earthworks. We would climb the trees and some were great for climbing. Branches were easy to reach and evenly spaced and allowed us to climb to the very top and look across the green canopy at the roofs of the houses. Great fun and I don't remember falling. Even more fun were crossbows. In the days I was at Harehills C.P. you could buy metal crossbows that fired wooden arrows with rubber suckers on the end. There was a thick black rubber band strung across the arms of the bow and this had to be pulled back, looped over a holder that was released when the trigger was pulled. The bows were green painted metal and could fire the arrows thirty to forty feet with quite a speed. We had good fun firing at each other and targets, which was pretty tame until we had better ideas. We decided we wanted the real thing and so we tried out darts from the dart board, sharp metal points variety. The largish darts fitted snugly into the groove where the arrow, or bolt, should go and when we shot the first one it was amazing. It flew straight, fast and far and stuck into a tree. This was magic! Instead of playing we now had the real thing. The only drawback, apart from the potential of killing someone, or putting out an eye, was that darts were so easy to lose in the undergrowth. We had such a great time and somehow we lived past childhood.

My father cleared the front and side of the house in Gipton Wood Crescent of trees so that he could have a drive built and the drive was then tarmacked. This provided a range of possibilities for young boys. We had been given roller skates, the kind that were extendable to fit your shoes and then strapped on. These were ok, but they had four wheels that would stick on a loose stone and send you head over heels. We decided on a better use for them and that was placing a hardbacked book on top of one, sitting on it and shooting down our driveway onto the road. It was good fun and we could get up quite a pace. There were some drawbacks, removing the skin off your knuckles as you held on to the book, removing the skin off your leg, if you fell off sideways and potentially being run over at the end of your run. None of these seemed to deter us and, in fact, spurred my brother and me to decide we could do better. I suppose we were partially inventing the skateboard. Just childhood pioneers, I guess. We travelled further afield to a much steeper hill. There was one just on the corner of Upland Crescent and Gipton Wood Avenue. The road suddenly fell steeply to the crossroads with Upland Grove.

The run would have been about fifty to sixty feet before you hit the crossroads and, of course, my brother was the first to give it a go. He set off, gained rapid pace, zigzagged and fell off sideways about half way down. I gave it a more tentative go and used my shoes as brakes to maintain a more modest speed. I think that by the end of the morning we had just about mastered getting a good run down the hill in one go. Luckily for us, there were few cars in our days, so the numbers of near misses at the crossroads were few.

My brother, Andrew, was always the most accident prone when we were children. School holidays seemed to last for ever and we had many adventures and even allowed my younger brother to join in as he got bigger.

TINKERS AND KITTENS

We moved to 19 Gipton Wood Crescent when I was younger than seven. I can't remember which year, but it was probably 1959 or 1960. The road was still cobbled in those days and it was only after we had been there a while that they came and tarmacked the centre of the road only leaving cobbles at the gutters on either side. The street was a hill that rose and fell from one side to the other and number 19 was just about at the summit. The houses were built before there were many cars and most only had a footpath leading up to them and ours was no different. All of them were semi-detached and ours was divided from the house next door by a row of trees. As we had a car one of the first tasks for my father was to build a driveway and garage so that the car could be brought off the street. Being practical and young, my father went about the task of cutting the trees down and removing the stumps and assorted bushes. This was quite a major task and my mother blamed it for my father's ill health a few years later.

Once the driveway was cleared then I remember workmen coming and laying a foundation and building a concrete garage. The garage was made of pre-formed concrete panels that were screwed together like a construction kit and the roof was probably asbestos. It was a very solid build and sat on a good concrete pad. They then laid the driveway and it was lovely black tarmac with white marble pieces. It looked very grand and, best of all, gave me and my brothers a lovely smooth surface to play on. The house was well above the street level so it had a steep hill at first and then levelled off. Prior to this we had

had to play in the street, but the drive gave us a new experience. It was great to run toy Dinky and Matchbox cars on and they shot down the drive, under the gates and onto the road at a great pace. It was also our cricket pitch. We did sometimes play on the road and we just had to stop play if a car or van appeared, but this wasn't very often. We still got 'rag and bone men' come collecting scrap metal and if there was any of value they may have paid a few pennies, but never very much. They came on a cart pulled by an old horse who must have done something wrong in a past life to have to suffer the dull existence. It would often have a nose bag on and when nature called left a little deposit of a warm smelly matter, which meant the cricket had to be abandoned as nobody was willing to remove it. My parents occasionally might collect it with the belief that it would be good for the garden. My wife tells me that her 'rag and bone men' in Stoke-on-Trent used to give goldfish as payment, but we never got anything as fancy.

This also reminds me that occasionally we would get knife grinders ride up the street. Most, I remember, came on a bike that had a grinding wheel attachment and they would sharpen your knives and scissors for a small fee. Nowadays, I don't know anyone who has knives sharpened unless they do it themselves. The other occasional visitors would be gypsies. A gypsy woman might knock on the door selling wooden dolly pegs. This always created excitement as they had a bad reputation and might put a curse on you if you didn't buy any. Mum was always friendly with them and their arrival seemed to coincide with the fair at Roundhay Park or at another venue.

Cricket on the road, when the surface had been tarmacked, was great. We would set up wickets, usually a cardboard box, and take turns. We needed some of the neighbours' kids to play with, as a well struck ball could shoot all the way down the road. The real problem with this playing in the street was the neighbour opposite. Miss Ellis lived directly opposite and she made it known very soon after we moved in that she did not like boys playing in the street or anywhere near her garden. She seemed very old to us, but maybe that was because everyone seems old when you're a child. Anyway, when the first ball was hit into her garden and my elder brother tried to get it, her front door opened and she marched out and told us in no uncertain terms that this would be the only time she would give us the ball back. She was true to her word and apart from lucky sorties, when we hoped she was out or not looking and managed to get in and out alive, she would keep any balls that strayed into her domain. She was the ogre of childhood stories, the witch that took little boys and cooked them, or at least she was to us. When I was older, I did cut her grass for a while and she wasn't quite as scary. I believe she was a piano teacher, but I never had lessons with her. She did want me to sing for her when I was teaching and she discovered I was in a production of Oliver as Fagin, but somehow I never found the time.

After our first encounter any shot into Miss Ellis's garden was six and out, and it was your responsibility to attempt to retrieve the ball. Failure signified the end of the game. The new driveway provided another venue without the same risk. The adjoining house was owned by a more approachable family. They had one son, Graham, and he was a bit older than us. The garage door provided a backstop and allowed just two to play. My brother and I could play for quite a time and as Boycott and Edridge were the cricketers we idolised, playing a 'dead bat' and developing our defensive style was quite important. For bowlers, the run up the steep drive was a challenge, but when releasing the ball on the flat, a fair head of steam could see bouncers thunder into the door. There were not the same problems retrieving the ball from next door, but if it entered on the full it was 'six and out'.

The slip fielder was a tiny gap between our garage and next door's. The space was about six inches and if the ball went in, a long stick or broom could retrieve the ball. Sometimes it was too far in and one of us, usually me as I was the smallest, had to squeeze into the space and retrieve the ball. It was very tight and scraped and removed skin, and very claustrophobic. When your head was in it was impossible to turn it around and you could only reverse blindly.

On one occasion, we all noticed quiet mewling sounds coming from the gap between the garages and we discovered that a cat had given birth to her kittens in the space. My mum was always very fond of animals and in some ways more than she was of humans, and I was sent in to retrieve them. I think Andrew might have tried first, but, as I said, he was too big and so I was given the task. The problem was that to grasp the tiny balls of fur, teeth and claws, I had to lower myself in the space so I could reach down to grasp them. This was very difficult, particularly as the kittens weren't too keen on being grasped, but I final managed to get the first and make my way out, only to have to repeat the procedure until all were rescued. The rescued cats were placed in a box and fed a saucer of milk, before being driven to the vet's for re-homing.

The driveway was steep enough to be a real challenge for getting the car up, but with barely a couple of inches on either side from the metal gate posts, my father developed the knack of coming in with surprising speed. At first the curb was a problem and he made wooden wedges to help the wheels get over the curb. Our playing space was taken when the car was in, but we developed a series of games for down the slope. It was a great space to race toy cars as I mentioned earlier, but when the wooden gutters were removed and replaced with plastic ones then the spare lengths of wooden gutters were even better for channelling the cars. We also had them jump over gaps and the crashes were brilliant.

We even managed to practise our tennis against the wall, which was challenging, as there were only about three and a half yards of driveway before entering next door. In a previous blog, I mentioned roller-skates and riding them whilst sitting on a book, but there was also the red metal scooter. These were fairly basic, but great fun, but suffered the same problem as the roller-skates as any stones would tend to make them stop dead and throw you over the handlebars. Children now have their BMXs, Hot Wheels, skateboards, electric toys, but it was much more fun when your imagination was left to create new games and toys and the world was your oyster. Even more magical was when it snowed, but that will have to wait for another time.

GETTING MOBILE AND STAYING THERE.

I guess that one of life's greatest pleasures was the ability to get around your world without having to be reliant on your parents.

As a child my first real means of getting around and the thrill of speed came from my scooter. Now scooters in the 1950s were not the flash modern ones used to perform aerial tricks, but rather the red painted things with two wheels about five inches in diameter, with hard rubber tyres. It was never a smooth ride, but with a slope you could pick up a speed. They were equipped with a heel brake which was basically a lever that when pressed put friction against the wheel and hopefully slowed you down. Use of the scooter wasn't aided by rough surfaces of the roads and pavements. I enjoyed riding mine down Lawrence Avenue, but it only took a small pebble to get under the front wheel to bring the scooter to a complete stop and for you to pile off head over heels. The result was often a grazed knee, some blood and the need for mum's care with washing it clean and applying the magic Germolene cream.

Whilst we lived in Lawrence Avenue my brother had a tricycle. Now this wasn't one of the modern things that toddlers have, this was a mean machine. It had large spoked wheels, about eighteen inches in diameter, with proper ball-bearing axles and chain and pedals. You can probably still get them, but at that time they were common. The major advantage of these was that they were real bikes that could get up a good head of speed and had a great turning circle, without the risk of tipping over. They also allowed a passenger. Someone could stand on the top of the rear axle and hold onto the shoulders of the rider. We used it a lot and it gave us the first taste of speed, danger and adventure whilst riding. I am not sure why they fell out of fashion, maybe they were too fast for younger children. They did have good brakes, but like Robin Reliants they could turn over if you tried to turn a corner too quickly.

Whilst remembering Lawrence Avenue, I recalled the old slag-heap that was nearby, on the left at the bottom of the road. It was fenced, but there were gaps through the chainlink that no one seemed bothered about. This heap gave me my next taste of adventure with speed. Kids used to slide down the slope, much like sledging. Old metal trays and even bonnets off cars were used and it really was life-threatening to hurtle down the coal heap at break-neck speeds and have to throw yourself off before you hit the fence at the bottom or hit a gap and hurtled onto the road. I think I only used the abandoned car bonnet once as that really had the potential to kill you.

The journalist and writer, Bill Naughton, wrote a series of short stories called Spit Nolan and Other Stories. It is a wonderful book that tells of life in the 1930s and is full of real characters. Spit Nolan is a boy who is the champion trolley rider. We would call them bogeys in Leeds. The bogey was a homemade vehicle and was basically a plank of wood with large wheels on a fixed axle at the rear, a thin plank which reached out that held a cross plank near the front. This cross piece had another axle and two smaller wheels. The cross plank was held by a nut that allowed it to move, so that you could steer the front wheels. Many kids had them in the 1950s and my dad made one for my brother and me. More often than not they had pram wheels and these allowed great speeds to be reached on a downward slope. I think my dad had the basic wooden structure made at his works, Catton's Steel Foundry on Black Bull Street near the River Aire in Leeds.

Our bogey didn't have pram wheels and it wasn't as fast as it could have been. Looking back, I realise that that was most likely deliberate on my dad's part. He didn't want us killing ourselves. This probably also explained why the wooden sledge he made for us didn't have metal runners. It had wooden runners that we rubbed a wax candle on to make them slippy. Again, it never was as fast as it could have been. The bogey, though, worked fairly well and it could fit my brother and me on it and we used it rather like a bobsleigh. One of us would be in the steering position at the front and the other, usually me, pushed from behind and when the speed built up you had to jump on behind the driver. I well remember rattling down Lawrence Avenue, trying to dodge pedestrians, bins and assorted children and onlookers. The roads were much quieter and there were few cars, so the road was often used. I believe there were others in the street with bogeys and races used to take place. I know ours was neither the best nor the fastest, but it was still great fun. I can still hear the whoops and cries of joy as we hurtled like charioteers down the pavements and roads. Yes, there were accidents, whenever my elder brother was involved, there were accidents. I always seemed to get away with it, but he seemed to attract them. At least, that was the case until I got older.

Shortly after my younger brother was born, we moved to Gipton Wood Crescent and it was there that I got my first two-wheeler bike. My mum got it for me second-hand and I can still vividly remember my first attempt at riding it down the street. I am sure that Miss Ellis, who lived across from us, must have been livid. I think that a family with three boys moving in opposite must have caused her great distress, particularly when we played in the street. On my bike I could only just manage to touch the ground on one side with the tip of my toe, but that was enough. I was given a push and I wobbled at bit, managed to get my foot onto the pedal, push the pedal and suddenly I was off down the slope. Now it would have helped if someone had given me better instructions on how to stop. Moving quicker by the moment, due to the momentum, I realised I didn't know what to do. I had been shown the brakes and I just pulled hard on them. Luckily I pulled both, or I would have gone over the handlebars if I had just pulled the front wheel brake. I came to a stop, wobbled again and fell sideways. It was a very undignified ending to my first ride and the rough road hurt and grazed my legs as I was lying on the side still astride the bike. It didn't help that I, like all boys at that time, was wearing shorts, which left flesh exposed to the hard surfaces. Boys' legs in particular, all these years later, still have scars and blemishes that tell the story of their childhood adventures and misadventures. (My wife tells me girls' legs too.) As you do if you fall off a horse, I got straight back on, after pushing the bike back up the slope to my house. The assorted onlookers were there to observe my second attempt. There does seem a certain human pleasure in watching the misfortune of others and why would they miss this opportunity? A growing crowd of local children had appeared like magic and there was pressure put on me not to embarrass myself or my family by failing to master riding a bike.

The second go was similar to the first, but this time the ride ended much more sedately with me braking and managing to get my foot on the ground and not falling. The crossbar did administer considerable pain to my anatomy, and to this day I do not understand why bikes in these times were built gender specific. Girls had bikes without the crossbar which made mounting and dismounting easy. Boys' bikes had the cross bar that must have caused untold injuries to male riders and possibly resulted in a drop in the number of children being born. Anyway, my second ride proved uninteresting to the onlookers and I was left alone to hone my riding skills. Within a matter of a few days, I was a dab hand at riding and a new world was beckoning. The first avenue for me to develop and experience adventure was the Little Wood, between the houses in the Easterlies and Gipton Woods. I believe the land was given for community use and is still there. It had a few trees and what we called the bomb hole. I have no idea if the crater was the result of a bomb, but it provided a great space to ride down the very steep slope and jump over bumps, logs and roots and take off and land, much like motorbike scramblers. We were not the first and weren't the last to use the wood in this way. The bike tracks were well worn and it was possible to race others as you mastered the rugged terrain. The first time you rode down the steepest bank and stayed on your bike was a moment of pride and accomplishment, as was the first time that your bike left the ground. It was such a wonderful place to play. We spent hours, days and years just living with wild abandon.

From the Little Wood we took our bikes to Gipton Wood and there we had a much larger area to explore. I remember well riding up and down the banks of what I only recently realise was a very old historical remains of an Iron Age camp.

Parenting was truly different and we only had to return for meals or when it got dark. Bikes gave us the freedom to explore the wider world, and Roundhay Park, Shadwell and beyond became our playground. I still remember riding out to find some of the best conkers, sheltering under trees with our bikes during thunder storms and having picnics. Bikes, and certainly those with gears, gave us these opportunities, as did quiet roads and parents who weren't overly anxious. Cities have become more dangerous places and unfortunately children nowadays don't have the luxury of exploring the world as we did. Guess we were just lucky!

GONE FISHING, HOOK, LINE AND SINKER!

I had better start off by saying that I have never had any success as an angler, and probably that is a term I shouldn't use when describing myself. My earliest experiences were at Roundhay Park Little Lake, where my elder brother and I would have nets fixed on long cane poles. The nets were a green mesh and we would trawl along the edge of the lake, seeing what we could discover lurking in the olive green depths. Usually, the results were weed and little else, but occasionally we would discover minnows and the odd stickleback. We would be equipped with the obligatory jam jar so that we could fill it with water from the lake and we could keep our prizes. Understanding of the environment was very different in the late 1950s early 60s and no one ever suggested that it was wrong. We would keep one or two of the fish we caught and took them back to our house. Unfortunately these beautiful, tiny creatures had about the same life expectancy as the goldfish from the fairs and would not live beyond a day or two. Of course, we were not the only children doing this and the accumulative effect would have been great.

The same occurred with frog spawn. Children collected it and often took it home. We placed the spawn in an empty goldfish tank and after a few days we saw the spawn hatch and the tadpoles appear. There were large numbers of these tiny black creatures swimming in the tank. Over time, the numbers decreased as some got bigger and we realised they were eating the others. Back legs developed and they got bigger still, and of course, the numbers decreased even further. Finally, we were left with froglets and dad took us to Hetchel woods where we put them back into the dam to give them a chance. Today, the collecting of spawn is banned and for good reason, as frog numbers are becoming endangered.

Our early experience with fishing did not put us off and developed to the next level when we were both bought fishing rods. I am not sure if they were Christmas presents, but if they were I only ever remember going fishing when the weather was good. The rods were nothing like the carbon-fibre models of today, with fabulous spinning reels. No, these were cane and made of three pieces that fitted together with metal joiners. The eyelets were bare metal thread spliced onto the cane and the reel was a very basic round wheel with a handle. Even so, we were delighted. Dad took us on our first outing and we went to Collingham on the River Wharfe near Wetherby. Prior to going, we went to purchase a coarse fishing licence. Now, we had a couple of licences over our angling career, one from Frew's sports shop in Harehills and another from a newsagent's where Easterly Road becomes Wetherby Road at the bottom of Wellington Hill. My dad also bought maggots and my brother and I were fascinated by the crawling mass of grubs.

We arrived at Collingham and after a walk along the riverbank we found a spot that my father seemed to think would be a good place. We put the rods together and dad showed us how to thread the line, tie a hook, add floats and then lead balls as sinkers. The next bit was the one I hated and that was putting maggots on the hooks. The poor creatures just writhed in the box and I really didn't want to touch them. They had a strange smell and were like something out of a nightmare. Dad took one out and pierced it with the hook and then did a second one. It was horrible! They may not be much in the animal chain, but it seemed wrong to inflict pain on them. As you can tell, I was a bit sensitive at this age and probably still am. My elder brother did it, but I refused. Anyway, the hooks were baited and then dad showed us how to cast. He did it once or twice and then we had a go. It took quite a bit to master getting the line to flow and the hook to travel a suitable distance on to the gently flowing river. We tried to avoid weed and rocks and finally we had our lines out and the floats bobbed up and down. It was all so exciting, but then nothing. We waited expectantly for the fish to rush to our bait and seize the hook, but nothing happened. When you are under ten, waiting is not a good thing. It went on for an eternity. After a while, we wound our line in, re-baited the hooks and then dad cast mine out with great aplomb. Unfortunately as he whipped the rod back and forth the hook, maggots and all, caught me between the eyes and latched on. There was a sharp tug, and probably a cry from me, before dad realised what had happened. To my horror, apart from the pain, there was a hook lodged between my eyes and even worse, two maggots dangling there.

Hooks are designed to pierce, but the barb is there to prevent the hook being easily dislodged. Dad realised how close he had come to putting my eye out and attempted to remove the hook as quickly as possible. It may have been that another experience with my mother's displeasure, the incident after losing Sabot at the soccer, was still etched in his mind, that explained his urgency and panic. I, in return, was not happy about having more pain inflicted and did not stand there calmly, but writhed, making his attempts and probably the pain more severe. Finally, it was torn loose and after being told not to be a baby, we returned to fishing. The blood between my eyes had been wiped with a hanky dampened with a certain amount of spit.

After this experience I can't say that I was enamoured by this pastime, but we persevered for the rest of the afternoon. We didn't even get the excitement of a nibble. Knowing my father's game-keeping ancestry, I must say he was a bit of a disappointment in the angling department. We did return on several occasions and never did we threaten to catch any fish, but it was a peaceful way to spend time in beautiful surroundings, have a packed lunch and get fresh air. To be honest, I am not sure what we would have done if we had caught anything. My fishing ability seems to have been passed on to my sons and, in particular, the youngest. He has fished many times here in Perth, but has never brought anything home to show for his efforts.

A TRIP TO THE SEASIDE – THE EAST COAST

I am sure that one of the most vivid memories which readers who lived in Yorkshire during the 1950s and 1960s will have of childhood is going on day trips to the seaside. I say day trips rather than holidays as for many families, staying at hotels or guest houses was an expense that was beyond them. One of the benefits of living in Leeds is that it is almost equidistant from the east and west coasts of England. In a car it is a trip of an hour and a quarter to an hour and a half, but my first memory is of travelling by train to Scarborough. Not only was this a steam train, but it was also one with compartments, just like in the Agatha Christie novels. I believe the train went via York and the station at Scarborough was at the top of the town and meant quite a long walk to get to the beach. It was never a problem going to the sand, but the slog back up the hill on tired legs was an unpleasant end to the day.

I think we only did the train journey once as we were fortunate to get a car whilst living in Lawrence Avenue. If my memory serves me well, I believe it was the first car in the street. It was an old Austin and required the use of a starting handle. It had no heating and the family named it affectionately, The Fridge. Going anywhere in the car was an adventure, but that was because you were fairly likely to suffer a breakdown, particularly if the journey involved a lot of hills. The Fridge struggled with hills and would overheat. A number of forced stops were involved, allowing the engine to cool so that we could start off again. My dad was an engineer so he was fairly handy with the mechanics, but I don't think he enjoyed it. Eventually, either by increased income or sheer frustration, The Fridge was replaced by a Ford Prefect. As was the rule in these times, you could have any colour you liked as long as it was black. It was a bigger car and with a growing family it provided more comfort and reliability. It had running boards and headlights that sat on top of the mudguards with chrome surrounds. We did feel grand in it on our first trip.

It is staggering how life has changed. In the 1950s there were few cars and the roads were often deserted. Leeds was coming to the end of its tram service and cobbled roads were being covered in tarmac as there were few horse-drawn vehicles. Of course, there were no motorways and travelling was a slow but pleasant experience, unless you suffered travel sickness. My wife tells me the remedy for her family was to sit on a newspaper. I had never heard of this before, but she is from Stoke-on-Trent, not from God's Own Country, so maybe it was just one of their little quirks. The journey was dull and we had to play games to fill in the time. There were not even car radios in these times so I Spy, The Parson's Cat and assorted games were tripped out, along with Ten Green Bottles and eventually, I See the Sea, The Sea Sees Me. There was always a stop at some point as my older brother would be sick, much to my father's ire. Even barley sugars couldn't prevent it. I was just lucky and, unless I am reading, I never feel sick. Of course, the driver never suffers, it is only the passengers who are afflicted.

There would be bottlenecks where certain roads met on the journey. York was one, as was Tadcaster, but once past those, the roads were pretty clear. The most common trips were to Bridlington, Hornsea, Filey, Scarborough or occasionally Robin Hood's Bay and Staithes. We almost always went to the Yorkshire coast and we loved to go. If you set off fairly early, you could be there by mid-morning and, leaving at about 4.00pm, you could be home in time to go straight to bed.

Once the trip was planned then nothing, including storms was going to stop us. For those not acquainted to Yorkshire weather, it usually rains or drizzles throughout the summer or at least it seemed to. On some occasions the sky would be blue, the temperature hot all the way to the outskirts of Scarborough, but as you hit the town it disappeared in a thick sea fret (fog). I didn't know why at the time, but now realise it is due to a temperature inversion. Whatever the reason, it would hang around all day and put a real dampener, literally, on the trip. Of course, just to rub it in, the fret would vanish as you left the town on the car ride home.

There was a ritual to going to the seaside that lasted beyond my childhood and my children's childhood and is probably still in existence today in the UK. The first thing was to find a car park, and on a busy bank holiday that usually meant a fair way away from the beach front. We carried bags with packed lunches from the car and headed towards the coastal front. On the way, we had to purchase the essentials. These were spades and buckets, maybe some flags and often plastic sandals. Unfortunately it was often raining so there were plastic coats and sou'westers. Whatever the weather, we then headed to the front with great optimism. Two deckchairs would be hired, our spot on the sand selected and this often meant another long hike before my dad was happy and we would be settled for the rest of the day. On sunny days, because there was no need to purchase macs, we might be allowed to buy something else. I remember well the wooden yachts. They had solid wood bases, usually painted red. They came in several sizes and had a wooden mast and canvas sails and little strings to adjust and trim the sails. These were no use in the sea, but were ideal for the numerous paddling pools that seemed to be everywhere.

Mum and Dad would settle in the deckchairs and we boys would strip off to swimmers, weather permitting, and head for the sea. Now if you have ever been in the North Sea then you will know what I mean when I say that I have never experienced cold like it. It would cut like a knife and your feet would turn blue within minutes. Only the very brave, insensate or suicidal would venture beyond the knees and I was none of the above. After this, it was down to sandcastle construction. We would choose the ideal spot, begin to dig the moat and build up the castle mound in the process. The skill was picking the spot where the water was just below spade level. If you got it right the moat would hold water that you collected from the sea in one of the buckets. Shells were added for decoration and sand pies (that's what we called them) added around the wall and on the castle top. The making of these became quite a feat of engineering.

Wet sand had to be shovelled into the bucket, smoothed off with a spade, the bucket quickly inverted and tapped on the bottom a few times before you pulled it off, leaving the sand pie behind. If you had them, or found some around the sand, you could add a paper flag. There was great kudos in having the most architecturally pleasing castle and children would look on with envy at any particularly good specimens. Everyone would wait for the family of builders to leave so that you could be the first to jump on their creation and send it back to the sand it was constructed from. Another pleasure was fighting the tide. As the tide crept in, castles were at risk of being washed away (maybe a portent of future sea level rising due to global warming) and we would scurry to repair damage as the waves lapped at the walls and caused erosion in a frenzy of excitement. It was fabulous fun even though we felt like King Canute. Time and tide waits for no man and it certainly demonstrated that, as eventually our castle disappeared under the waves. This normally signalled the end of the day and time to set off home, but in between we would have lunch. The activity seemed to make us ravenous. Mum always had a packed lunch of beef paste, or fish paste sandwiches. Sometimes it was potted meat, but I never really liked them. Usually Mum and Dad would have a thermos of tea and they would read the papers in peace until we had finished our sandwiches. At this point there were cries of 'Ice-cream!' and one of us would go with mum or dad back onto the front to buy some 99s. (The Italian King had ninety-nine elite bodyguards and Italians called anything elite Ninety-nines) They were often starting to melt by the time we returned and after handing them out. Somehow sand would stick to the ice-cream, but we didn't care. You had to eat them quickly and lick any drips off the cone. Often I would bite the end of the cone off and suck the ice-cream-through the hole. The Flakes were lovely and I saved those to last.

As we grew, times and experiences changed and so did the seaside towns. They had had their heyday and were getting run down and shabby, but we didn't care. They were another world. Somehow the coast reminded me of the Secret Seven, or Famous Five stories by Enid Blyton and I imagined the fishermen could be smugglers, or the fairground workers spies. The fishing industry was still thriving with the cobble boats busy with small-scale fishing. It was so different from life in Leeds and I have many more tales to tell of visits to the Yorkshire coast.

CROWS NEST CAMP

Apart from the day trips to the coast, we did start to stay for longer periods, but I don't ever remember staying at a guest house or hotel in our younger years. I suppose the reason would have been expense. We did try camping one year and I believe that was at a site called Crows Nest and it was near Filey and Scarborough. I have checked and I think the site is still there. At the time, which must have been in the 1960s, I remember being very excited that we were going to go on holiday and that we would be camping. I have checked my photographs and found one with my mother sitting with a baby on the steps of a caravan, so what I think is that my parents and baby Stuart were in the caravan. My elder brother, Andrew, and I would have been in the tent as I don't ever remember staying in a caravan.

The car was packed and we set off from Leeds with great excitement and the usual routine of songs and games in the car. I believe Andrew managed his usual car sickness treat somewhere on the way, possibly York or near Tadcaster. I think that the car was a Ford Anglia and I know it was the first car my father bought that was new.

We thought it was a fantastic car, but looking back it was fairly sparse, with a small dashboard and mainly metal surrounds and I am not sure if it had seat belts. If it did, there certainly weren't any in the back. The seats were a slippery vinyl and on a hot day would stick to your bare legs. Despite these limitations, it was fantastic. It started first time, did not need a starting handle, it had a heater and I even think it had a radio, but I can't be sure. Anyway, somehow we all piled into it and the boot must have had the tent and everything else.

I believe additional storage was below our feet at the back of the front seats. I think we were only going for the weekend, but for us it was a real adventure.

We arrived in the evening and found our spot and settled in and explored whilst mum and dad unpacked the car and then we helped our dad set up the tent. At that time the site was really just an empty

Mum, Andrew, baby Stuart and me on the camping trip.

field, but there was a simple toilet block and I think you could go to the farmhouse to buy fresh milk. The tent we had was one Dad had borrowed and it was the old ex-army thick canvas type. There was no flysheet or built-in ground sheet, but there was a tarpaulin to separate us from the rough grass. Finding the right spot without large bumps and lumps was difficult, but eventually it was sorted and tea and a quick meal were produced using a primus stove. It was very basic and it seemed to take ages to conjure up beans on bread. We didn't care. It was all so exciting. The weather wasn't particularly good that Friday night and the temperature fell quickly and so eventually we were tucked up in our tent with a few blankets. I can't say that it was comfortable night and it was quite cold. We woke at first light and Andrew and I climbed out of our tent and wandered over to the toilets. Breakfast was cornflakes and milk and as soon as possible we set off in the car into Scarborough. We returned later in the afternoon with fish and chips and we had arranged to go on a Mystery Tour.

For the uninitiated, a Mystery Tour was a bus trip that you bought tickets for and had no idea where you were going, hence the mystery part. Families and couples would fill the coach or bus and off you would head out of the town, passing the wonderful scenery, maybe stopping off at some point of interest or two and then arriving at a pub with a beer garden. The adults would have a few drinks and the children would have a lemonade and maybe a packet of Smith's Crisps. There was only one flavour at that time and salt was provided in a little blue paper twisted bag. They tried to bring them back years later, but they were not the same as they didn't have the twist and were just sealed bags. After a short stop, we would all get back on the bus, the adults a little more chatty, and we would head back to the starting point. For some reason, there was always a whip-round for the driver and a collection would be made and someone would hand it to him before we all got off. The Mystery Tour became a regular part of our early holidays and it seemed to be more fun for our parents than us boys.

It was late when we got back to the site and we just piled back into the tent and had a more restful, if still uncomfortable night's sleep. The following morning was much sunnier and probably to get us out of the way, Dad took us for a walk. Crows Nest camp was perched high on the cliffs and the field had a wire fence and there was a footpath running along the cliff edge. At places, the path was very close to the edge and I was quite nervous so Dad held both our hands. I was on the field side against the fence, then there was my Dad, and Andrew was along the side nearest to the drop. I noticed that the fence was quite insubstantial and there were just two wires and metal poles at regular intervals. We were enjoying our walk and the field next to us was filled with a herd of black and white cows. The sun was out, there were fluffy white cumulus clouds and the sea was a vivid blue and there were white tops to the waves. Birds were circling and I think they were crows and there were some gulls and it was one of those days where everything was perfect. There was the smell of salt, fresh grass and wild flowers and we were enjoying our stroll. That was until I took hold of the fence. I don't know why I did it. It was there and maybe it was for security as we were close to the edge, but suddenly I felt a thump of power, a jolt through my hand and arm. I cried out and Andrew and Dad realised something wasn't right as they were shocked. It was so sudden Andrew nearly fell off the cliff edge. The fence was electrified to keep the cattle from wandering off the edge of the field. Apparently, there were some signs warning of this, but I had taken no notice. I was shocked, but no harm was done. It was the first of a number of times I have managed to electrocute myself.

Dad decided we should head back and we were very careful not to touch the fence again. Mum was ready for us and we started to pack the car. When everything was ready, we headed back into Scarborough and stopped off to buy a stick of rock each. The rock was bright red, mint flavoured and had the lettering of Scarborough all the way through it. They were wrapped in clear cellophane and there was a little black and white picture of a scene of Scarborough at the middle. They were wonderful and the trick was to suck them so that they lasted all the way home. We had no idea how they got the letters through them, but that was part of the mystery. I can taste them now as I am typing this. Mum and Dad didn't have rock, they had a packet of mint humbugs. We weren't allowed to eat them until we were heading back to Leeds and we spent the rest of the day cradling them whilst we went into a Penny Arcade. We were allowed so much money, two shillings seems about right, and we changed it into large penny coins. We then were in a world of lights, noise and pulling the handles of the machines that managed to take all of your money by the end, regardless of how much you won. It seemed that even then they had worked out how to ensure that no one left with any winnings, and we would just feed the machines until the pennies ran out and then look longingly at Mum and Dad, but rarely were we allowed any more.

Before we left Scarborough, we went into a cafe to have a proper fish and chip meal, with tea and bread and butter. The knives were unusual, the silver teapots and extra water were all part of the magic and the golden fish batter and chips were delicious with a squeeze of exotic lemon. The chip butties with melting butter were to die for, and many probably did. But, by golly, were they delicious!

Tired, full, we were driven back home. The car was quieter, with only the sucking rock noises. Later we drifted off to sleep, and at journey's end we were lifted out of the car and carried to our beds.

A TRIP TO SCARBOROUGH

It seemed that for most of my early life my parents took us to the seaside on either day trips or to stay in cottages they would hire. The main places to visit were Bridlington, Filey, Hornsea or Scarborough and it is Scarborough that I want to remember today. The journey time by car was about the same to all of these and was a journey of about an hour and a half. As an adult, this is just a short trip, but as a young child it seemed to last a lifetime. There was little to amuse us in the car unless we played our own games and, as discussed earlier, these involved, I Spy, the Parson's Cat and was supplemented by a range of songs. My mum and dad were probably getting pretty desperate by the time we arrived. Three young boys would have challenged the sanity of any parent and when the sweets ran out: barley sugars to help my elder brother not suffer car sickness; Mintoes, my dad's favourite; and Murray Mints, mine, there was nothing left but to squabble.

Scarborough was the largest of the Yorkshire seaside resorts and it had two bays. One was full of amusement arcades, donkeys on the beach, Punch and Judy shows and the like, whereas the other was much quieter and more genteel. A large ruin of Scarborough Castle stood partially collapsing into the sea, built to repel invaders and those from north of the border. Scarborough used to suffer an annual invasion from the Scots when their factories closed for Works Weeks and the masses descended onto the town. Scarborough was thriving in the late 1950s and early 60s, as continental travel had not really started and holiday camps, such as Butlins, were booming with organised holidays with a service to occupy children and allow adults a bit of peace.

Dad, Andrew and me at Peasholm Park, Scarborough.

Apart from the sea and sand and front amusements, Scarborough did offer other forms of entertainment. Peasholm Park had been opened in 1912 and it had ornamental gardens, which were of no interest to young boys, but it did have something that was. The lake was the scene of naval battles. The battle of the River Plate was re-enacted daily and large replica ships moved across the lake, cannons fired with real smoke and I believe it was narrated. I loved it! I did hear that the largest of the ships had people inside controlling them, but I have no idea if that was true. It was a real spectacle to watch and the lake was also a place where we could sail the new yachts that we had just bought. The yachts were wooden boats, brightly painted and had real canvas sails and little strings to pull and trim the sails. We mainly sailed them in small pools so that we wouldn't lose them if they took off with the wind. They were great fun and returned home with us to sail in the bath. One other part of the park I loved was a night visit to the illuminated island. The park was set out as an oriental garden and at night you could pay to cross the arched bridge and enter a world of magic. Well, it seemed so. On the island were characters from Walt Disney and these were lit from inside and it was magical seeing Snow White and the Seven Dwarfs standing in the foliage illuminated from within.

Another place we would visit was Oliver's Mount where the motorcycle racing took place. We would drive around the course and imagine what it would be like to drive it in a race. We would then go to The Mere. The Mere is a large ornamental lake with nice walks and a café. Why would this interest young boys, you might ask? Well, when we used to go, there was a pirate galleon, the Hispaniola , and if we were good we would set sail and land at an island in the lake and here we were set loose to hunt for buried treasure. The pirate crew were a very motley bunch and dressed the part. They would ham up the acting, check their maps and encourage us to scavenge for gold coins. I never found one, despite several visits, but many years later I took my eldest son back when he was about four or five, and on this occasion he was successful and somewhere we probably still have the coin. I hope Long John Silver doesn't want it back! I believe that the Hispaniola has sailed off into the sunset, which is a shame. I am sure that many youngsters would still get a thrill from searching for lost treasure on a desert island.

Our final change of venue was the outdoor swimming pool. In the days when we went, the water was icy. The pool is now geothermally heated and, I am sure, much more pleasant. The weather on the Yorkshire coast is rarely hot and even when the rest of the area was bathed in sunshine, it wasn't unusual for Scarborough to be blanketed in a sea fret. The damp mist had a chill that would have prevented anyone daring to take a plunge. Most visits to Scarborough were spent either fully jumpered up on the sand, digging our way to China, or sitting in the car with the windows steamed up and a constant drizzle preventing us from venturing out. This was often accompanied by the smell of vinegar as we would eat fish and chips from the newspaper. I can taste them as I write this now. This was often accompanied with a 99 ice cream for dessert. However, on the one time we went to the outdoor pool, the weather was glorious. In these times, shortly after the war, no one was aware of sun damage and having a tan was the height of showing that you had been on a holiday and had a great time. When lotions were used, only by my mother, they tended to be coconut oil and I think the purpose was to assist in the frying. My mother would tan, but my brothers and I took after our dad, who was from Scotland, near Oban, and the Viking descent offered no protection from the sun's rays. The chill of the water disguised some of the burning and by the end of the day in the pool we were all like lobsters. I believe this was just a day trip and so we had a very uncomfortable ride back to Leeds. The shirts, so soft on the way, were now like ragged sandpaper and every movement brought groans.

When we arrived home, we were liberally padded down with calamine lotion and I can still smell the pink flowery smell. The cool touch was wonderful, but was short lived. We were put to bed and despite the pain, we all three managed to sleep. The worst was yet to come! The next day the soreness was less, but by the evening it was replaced by the itching. Again, more calamine lotion was added and it did provide temporary relief, but within moments the itching returned with a vengeance. We were instructed not to scratch it, but I challenge anyone to not scratch even a mild itch, yet alone an all-encompassing, mind numbing itch that would not go away. We scratched and scratched ourselves until, the following day, the inflammation began to subside, but small white blisters appeared and then finally the skin began to peel. At least two days of the itching was endured before our skin was replaced and the horror left us in peace. Of course, I now understand the dangers of the sun, living in the skin cancer capital of the world, but times were different. The English rarely had the weather to worry them until the advent of holidays in Europe and the guarantee of sunny holidays. You can tell the English tourists here in Perth, Western Australia, as they are the ones with almost transparent bodies that suddenly turn to lobster red.

THE ELEVEN PLUS

For keen parents in the 1960s, there was one thing in primary schooling that they desired and that was for their children to pass the Eleven Plus. Now for those who don't know, the Eleven Plus was a selection examination which was introduced after the war in 1944. Prior to this, there were direct-grant grammar schools that were largely independent, offering some scholarship places. Maintained grammar schools that were fully part of the state system came with the introduction of the Eleven Plus, and state education provided three alternatives: there were grammar schools, secondary modern schools and technical schools.

In order for me to explain the change I must take you back to my mother and her sister. As mentioned in another tale, they were born in the British Men's Institute, a snooker and whist club in Chapel Allerton. My mum's older sister, Joan, was a very capable student and was offered a full scholarship to attend a direct-grant grammar school, which she did. My mother in her turn, another capable student, also did well, but was only offered a partial scholarship to the grammar school. The result was that my mother never went, as my grandparents could not afford even half the fees. My mother ended up leaving school at 13 years old and went to work in the offices at the Railways in Leeds. Thirteen was the usual age to leave schooling for the majority of children and only those most capable went further. She met my father, an engineer at Catton's Foundry on Black Bull Street and they married. Immediately after they married, she lost her job at the Railways. The reason for this was they expected that once you were married you would start having children. In these times, there was no maternity benefit and very few workers' rights.

Aunty Joan and Mum as little girls.

There certainly was no sense of female equality, at least not in the working classes. Women were expected to have children and that was considered their role in life. In reality, my mother worked most of her life, as well as raising three boys. After they got married, my parents were living in a flat at the back of the shops at Oakwood, next to Gipton Wood, and the moment she became pregnant with my elder brother, they had to leave the flat. Again, there was no system to protect tenants and it was just the way it was. Luckily for my parents, my dad's job was a good one and they bought their first house, 36 Lawrence Avenue.

My mother valued education. She saw it as a way to escape poverty and she and my father had high aspirations. It was because of this that they scraped together the money to send, first Andrew and later me, to private preparatory school. She wanted to give us the best opportunities and she saw that as part of the way to do it. My brother went to a little school near the Methodist Church near Ladywood at Oakwood on the recommendation of a friend at the church, but the school closed and my brother and I attended Stainbeck Preparatory School until that too closed, due to the death of the headmistress, Mrs Genge. My elder brother left earlier than I did as he reached secondary age, and he attended Harehills Secondary Modern School. My mother was worried for his future, but she needn't have been, as he left Harehills after O'Levels and went to Allerton Grange and then to university and spent his working life teaching.

I started at Harehills County Primary at the age of eight and spent my Eleven Plus years with Mr. Kelly (1965 and 1966). Harehills was streamed at this time and Mr Kelly took the top class. Our parents had to buy three books of test papers in Arithmetic, English and General Problem Solving (an intelligence test) and we would practise these each week under test conditions. It is due to these tests that we learned numerous collective nouns and other information that is handy for crosswords, but not a great deal else. I don't remember being stressed by these and I rather enjoyed doing them. I can only think that Mr. Kelly must have loved the silence whilst we all did the tests and I don't think he marked them. I believe that we must have marked our own or each other's maybe. We spent weeks doing these and there was a build up to the test date and I know my mother was becoming stressed, but I don't remember us worrying. For the tests themselves, I believe all the classes came together into the hall. We sat in rows and alphabetically. I think it was all done on one day, but I could be wrong there. This was quite a big day in the school and all the classes that surrounded the hall had to be very quiet, on pain of death from their teachers. There were test booklets and we were instructed how to fill in the covers and then sit until we were given the command to start.

EDUCATION DEPARTMENT
CALVERLEY STREET
LEEDS. 1

J.H.TAYLOR, T.D., M.A.
CHIEF EDUCATION OFFICER
TELEPHONE NO. 35361

IN REPLY PLEASE QUOTE
S/PB/JB/4

6th May, 1966.

Dear Sir/Madam,

I am writing to inform you that the examination held recently indicates that a grammar or technical course is appropriate for your son.

This type of education is provided at Roundhay School where there is a place available for him. You will recall that you gave this school as your first choice.

I shall be glad if you will indicate on the slip below whether you wish to accept this place. I must emphasise that if you do accept this place you must allow your son to remain at school for at least five years and that the Education Committee reserve the right to transfer him at any time if, in their opinion, his progress is unsatisfactory.

Yours faithfully,

J. H. Taylor

Chief Education Officer

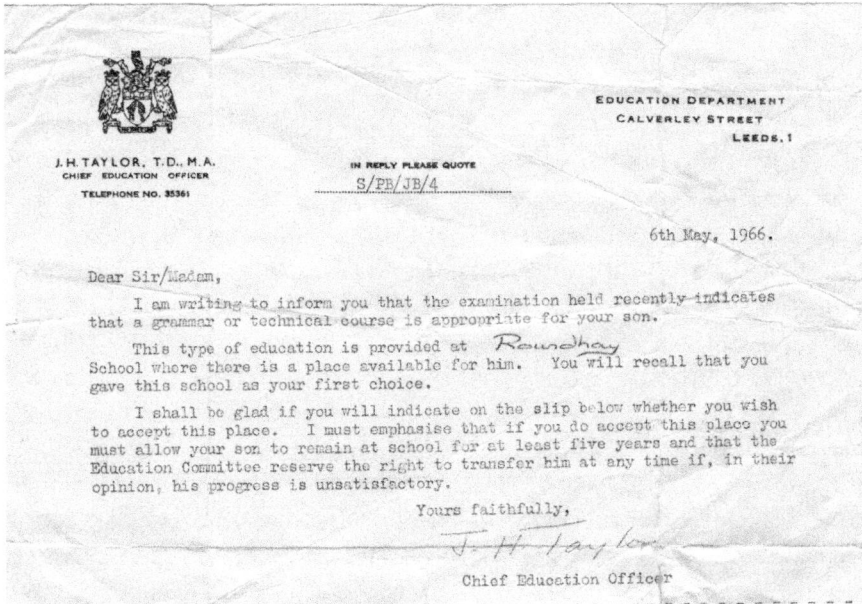

When the word was given, we set about it. We had been told many times that if you had spare time, to go back through the test to see if you had missed anything out. It didn't matter when you finished, you had to remain where you were in silence until the end of the time. At the end of the test, we went out for playtime and there was a lot of chatting, nervousness and comparing of answers. In a short time, we were back and ready to start the second paper. By the time we had finished them all, we were quite tired. Writing for so long was hard on your hands and wrists, but I can't remember any other stress. Afterwards, we had to face the cross-examination by our parents, where the usual answer of 'It was ok!' didn't seem to satisfy my mum. The next day we had forgotten all about it and school returned to normal, but without the regular practice tests. Somehow my mother knew the day the results were to come out and she told me to come straight home. Mr. Kelly appeared towards the end of the day with a pile of envelopes. I seem to remember we had forty-one in the class and the envelopes were addressed to our parents, but we were allowed to look at them. There was no question of pass or fail on the letter, but it said,

'I am writing to inform you that the examination held recently indicates that and grammar or technical course is appropriate for your son. This type of education is provided at Roundhay School where there is a place available for him.'

Now I seem to recall that all but four children received the same letter. Mr. Kelly took the other four to talk to them and I suppose he was being kind. The rest of us chatted and were quite excited. Some of my friends were also going to Roundhay School, or to the girls' school next door. I am trying to remember and I know John S, Richard B and Dick R went with me to Roundhay. I am sorry for those I have forgotten. It was the end of the afternoon and some of us had a mixed netball game after school in the girls' playground. I don't know why it was arranged for that day and it was boys versus the girls. The game was good; we beat the girls and then set off home. My letter was in my satchel, and when I approached my house on Gipton Wood Crescent, my mother was waiting outside, almost hysterical. I think she thought I had, in her words, 'Failed' and didn't want to come home. In reality, I had just forgotten all about it at that point.

Needless to say, she was delighted at the result and I was allowed to buy a toy from Varley's toyshop at Harehills. That weekend I did. I bought an Action Man, later called GI Joe. It was when they had just been released and they had appeared on Blue Peter. That was about the height of my excitement. I did hear some friends had bicycles, with gears and all sorts of things. I can only think they had more affluent families.

My mother quickly signed the acccptance slip and I returned it to school the next day. After that I forgot all about it until much nearer to leaving Harehills CP School.

LEEDS EDUCATION COMMITTEE

HAREHILLS COUNTY PRIMARY JUNIOR MIXED SCHOOL

Name *David Cameron* Class *HK* Date *Feb 1966*

SUBJECT		Class Tests Marks		Remarks
Reading	Oral	10	8	*Very good result*
	Comprehension	20	18	
English	Essay	20	12	*Spelling !!! He now tries*
	Usage	20	15½	*& is improving. Must not get discouraged.*
	Spelling	18	3½	
Arithmetic	~~Tables~~	20	25	*Generally good. Silly mistake in test.*
	Problems	20		
	Mechanical	30	20	*Should have done better. Careless.*
Handwriting		10	6	
Constructional Drawing		10	4	Final Position in Class Tests ...*24/41*...

Art, Craft, ~~Needlework~~. *Bags of ideas. Technique Improving.*

Social Studies. *A very interested worker.*

Physical Education. *Very good. A bit nervous in agility work*

General Remarks. *David works hard. A dependable boy.*

AGE GROUP GRADING (A – E)

Reading .... *A* ......   Mental Arithmetic .. *A* ....

English .... *A* .....   Mechanical Arithmetic .. *B* ....

Class Teacher. *K Kelly*   Headmaster. *Harold E. Nelson*

Signature of Parent. — *J E Cameron*

Age Group Grading.

This grading is intended to give an indication of your child's attainment in his/her age group regardless of the class in which your child is placed. This scheme of grading is dependent upon the following distribution:-

Grade	Indication	Approx. % in Age Group.
A	Very good	5
B	Above average	20
C	Average	50

SPORT AND THE FACTS OF LIFE

I always enjoyed sport at Harehills. I think it was mainly on a Wednesday afternoon, but I could be wrong. Maybe that was just when I was in Mr. Kelly's Yr. 4K class. Anyway, as the school was devoid of any green space to play, we would be greeted during lunch time by the arrival of, I think, two double-decker buses to ferry a host of excited and noisy children to the Soldiers' Field sports ground. The journey wasn't more that about ten minutes at most.

As I was thinking about this the other night, I pictured the ride and what we passed on the way. Just on the City side of the school was the family doctor's: Drs. Black, Freeman, Nevis and at least one other. I could be wrong with some of the names, but Dr. Black was a definite. My mother thought the young doctor was lovely and so he became ours whenever possible. It was strange, but many years later, when she had retired, she would babysit for his son, but the daughter then was a teenager and really didn't require care. Dr. Black also makes an appearance as the doctor in Wickergate, my first novel.

As the bus left the school, there was a zebra crossing and directly on the other side of the road was a sweet shop/tobacconist. This was the source of a range of lollies that will form another tale and the source of whip 'n' tops, yo-yos, skipping ropes and marbles. On the school side, I remember an old fashioned clothing shop. It ran a little way along the side road and sold Clarks Shoes and Ladybird children's clothes. I can't remember the name. Next to this was the Conservative Club, which I can't believe would still be there and above it was Olga Shear's Ballroom. I only went once for dancing lessons when I was about eleven. It seemed very old-fashioned and frightening and I never returned after that first go. This probably saved a lot of toes from being trodden on! I do remember a large net suspended over the dance floor that was full of balloons. I supposed they released them towards the end of an evening, but I never experienced that. Further along, on the other side, there was an antique/junk shop and it was there that my first and only violin was purchased. I believe there was an electrical shop and back towards school, a gent's barber shop.

There originally were three cinemas in Harehills. The Clock Cinema was the biggest and the newest and the building still remains, but there was one in the centre of Harehills, I think where the supermarket was built called The Harehills and one on the school side, but nearer to the city called The Gaiety Kinema, but that closed in 1958. It was replaced with a modern, large pub that developed a bad reputation and was later closed down.

On the junction with Harehills Road, there were shops I remembered well as they were a source of pleasure. One I believe was called Frew's and sold sports gear, and couple of shops up was the toy shop, Varley's, and I bought Airfix Kits there. Across from these was a Pet Shop and I always loved looking in the window at the animals and next to that was a café that my mum would occasionally take me and my two brothers to and when I was a teenager I sometimes went there.

The bus ride took us past the roundabout that had Easterly Road running off up the hill, but we carried straight on and passed the Astoria Ballroom, then Turnways Garage and next to it the Olympia Works. Originally, this was an aircraft factory and the Soldiers Field was a landing strip, but when I was a boy it was no longer a factory, but the buildings housed several small workshops and businesses. I do know that behind it up the hill, hidden in the woods, were aircraft shelters and I did explore these as a child. I am sure they are filled in now for safety. The works are now the Tesco building and there is a blue plaque there.

On our short journey, we passed Gipton Woods on the right and the tram lines ran all along the route, before their removal in the mid 1950s. We passed through Oakwood and turned up by the Oakwood Clock. The road ran next to it then and then up to the Soldiers' Fields, where they stopped and we poured out. Here we played soccer, cricket and I think we did athletics, but I can't remember much about it. I do remember one or two cricket matches with other schools, but I don't think we did a great deal of inter-school sport.

Soccer was hordes of us chasing a ball around with no sense of positions. The balls were heavy leather and, when wet, weighed a ton. Woe betide anyone who was unlucky enough, either by design or error, to head a wet ball. If the skull wasn't fractured, severe concussion was the likely outcome. Soccer boots, for those fortunate to have them, were heavy leather affairs, with leather studs nailed into the sole. The toe cap was a large, heavy, rounded end that really allowed no control as to the destination of the ball. If you enjoyed running and playing it was great, but for those less inclined to sport it must have been agony, standing, freezing in the cold. This, added to the embarrassment of being the last to be chosen for a team, must have caused some children to be emotionally scarred for life. The ultimate insult was when the last player was rejected by both teams; in this case the child would be sent to be the goalkeeper and if a goal was scored he was chastised by all his side, even when there was nothing he could have done to prevent it.

When the games session had finished, we all piled back onto the buses and headed back to school, all with differing versions of whether it had been an enjoyable experience or not.

And now the Facts of Life! One morning in Mr. Kelly's class Neil, I won't say his surname, came in excited. He told a group of us how babies were produced and there was considerable squirming as he told us. I was incredulous and full of disbelief. He was either making it up or mistaken. The word went around the class and I led the side disclaiming what he said. Babies were made by kissing, I proclaimed. Probably as it seemed the more likely, safe and acceptable theory, we had a vote and I was successful in winning the day. My debating skills were victorious, but it proved the first of many occasions where I didn't know what I was talking about. What also should have warned me was that I had been to more than one birthday party, where at a lull in proceedings the game of Postman's Knock was suggested and the chosen one would leave the room, numbers were issued to the other gender present and when this was done, the one outside returned. This person said a number and the owner of the number left the room to kiss the other who had chosen them. No one had ever fallen pregnant from playing the game as far as I was concerned!

THE PERILS AND PITFALLS OF SWIMMING LESSONS.

I briefly raised the subject of swimming lessons in an earlier tale, but I would like to return to it, as it was one of the areas of my life that I have found challenging. I have always been fairly sporty, but swimming was never my thing and it has given me an insight into how other children have to face activities they find challenging.

Swimming! It is one of those things, like reading, riding a bike, driving a car that there is one moment when you realise that you can actually do it. Prior to that point, it was an unbelievably difficult skill. I can still remember the time that I grasped the concept of division, the very moment when it suddenly seemed so obvious and I couldn't understand how I hadn't seen it before. Anyway, swimming! There were swimming pools, but in the 1950s I had never been to one and whereas I had paddled in the sea on the Yorkshire east coast, I had never been above knee deep and never for very long, as your legs would turn blue from the cold and lose all sense of feeling within a very short time.

Whilst at Harehills County Primary School, I started swimming lessons. I am not exactly sure which year we started, but I suspect it was third year with Mr Kelly. I know that I was quite anxious about it as I had never been in a pool before, but the day of reckoning was approaching and my fear was growing. It was a mixture of excitement and worry that I wouldn't be able to do it. The day arrived and I had a bag with my swimming trunks and towel and I walked down Easterly Road to school. I guess I was ten years old and I have been racking my brain which baths we went to. For some reason I seem to recall two. One was on Meanwood Road and Kirkstall Road also come to mind.

The first time we went is quite vivid and I remember the classes getting on a double-decker bus outside the school. If you were lucky you were allowed upstairs, but if not, you were sent downstairs. The buses upstairs held the lingering smell of stale tobacco. The upstairs gave a strange perception of overhanging the rest of the bus as you looked down. The best upstairs seats were right at the front and you got a great vantage point, but the movement and swaying of the bus was exaggerated and combined with the smell, had a tendency to make you feel sick. The seats were paired benches with fairly hard, marked, brown leather, or carpet-like upholstery. There was a chrome rail across the back of the bench and it was necessary to hold on to it as you moved about when the bus was in motion. Going down the stairs, whilst the bus was moving, was also challenging and added to the excitement.

Rolled towels and trunks were clasped to our knees and the journey was only short. We arrived and lined up outside the baths. The building was old then and I remember, not sure if this was both pools or just one of them, that there were cubicles on either side of the pool. The boys were down one side and the girls on the other. We were sent down our side and with our partners we had to change. This was a bit embarrassing as I wasn't used to public nudity, or at least with a boy from class, and it was very cold. The air in the baths had a strong cloying smell of chlorine and there was a strange echoing sound. Our trunks donned, shivering, we left the cubicle and faced the world. We had to line up at first and lift our feet up to have them inspected. Apparently, they were checking for verrucas, but I had no idea what they were.

Mr Kelly shouted orders and instructions and we were then divided into non-swimmers and those who claimed to be able to swim. Obviously, I was in the former group. Being quite good at sport, this was a new experience for me and at that moment I harboured unpleasant thoughts, blaming my parents for the ignominy and embarrassment. Why hadn't they taken me swimming before? Why hadn't I had lessons? Pool staff took some of the swimmers to one end, the deep end, of the baths and checked to see if they were swimmers and to group them further. My group was herded down to the shallow end for our first time in the water. There were stainless steel ladders and we were told to climb in and move to the end of the pool where there was a gutter. I became horrified and when my turn came, I started down the ladder and when the cold water hit the top of my legs, I froze. It was horribly cold. Mr Kelly saw my distress and approached it with his usual subtlety, told me to not be a baby and get in. Left with no choice other than total embarrassment, and certainly I wasn't brave enough to refuse his orders, I got in. The water reached to chest-height, just about armpit level and I grabbed the gutter with a strength that probably cracked the tiles. I clung on as if my life depended upon it and I thought it did. We pathetic creatures hung along the edge in the shallow end and were instructed to hold on the side and let our legs float. "As if?" My legs weren't coming off the bottom for anyone, but one by one we were inspected to see if we had achieved it. I watched the teacher getting nearer and I panicked. It was like waiting for the moment of doom. As I said, I had always been one of the sporty ones and I had never suffered the disgrace of being near the end when teams were picked for soccer, cricket or any games. We sniggered at those poor souls and, at the end, the last one was further belittled by the team refusing them and giving them to the other side. Here I was, equally suffering and I realised how it must have felt for them.

My turn came and I was told to let my legs float up. Somehow, one leg managed it, but the other was stuck to the floor. I was given further gentle encouragement of, "Get on with it, lad!" and finally, somehow my foot slipped and it floated up. The problem was, I got a mouthful of the foul water and immediately writhed, trying to regain my footing and coughing and spluttering. This was not my finest moment! I was bypassed for the next and, bit by bit, we were instructed to try and raise our legs, relax and then kick them. I eventually managed to do this and we were all in a line kicking and splashing great fonts of water everywhere, creating a racket. I was actually enjoying this, but by now I was getting very cold and I was relieved when a whistle was blown and we had to get out and get changed.

This should have been simple, but we were cold and shivering and the trunks didn't want to come off easily or the undies go on effortlessly. Added to that, we were all trying to hide our private parts from each other and there wasn't much space. To be honest, we were barely dry and it was a very raggedy looking mob of boys that appeared, whereas the girls seemed almost pristine and calm in comparison. We had to line up by the entrance when we were ready and then the teachers checked the cubicles and appeared with a wide array of towels, trunks and, in one case, a pair of underpants. It was funny how no one seemed to be missing them, but eventually the miscreant was tracked down by great detective work and his public

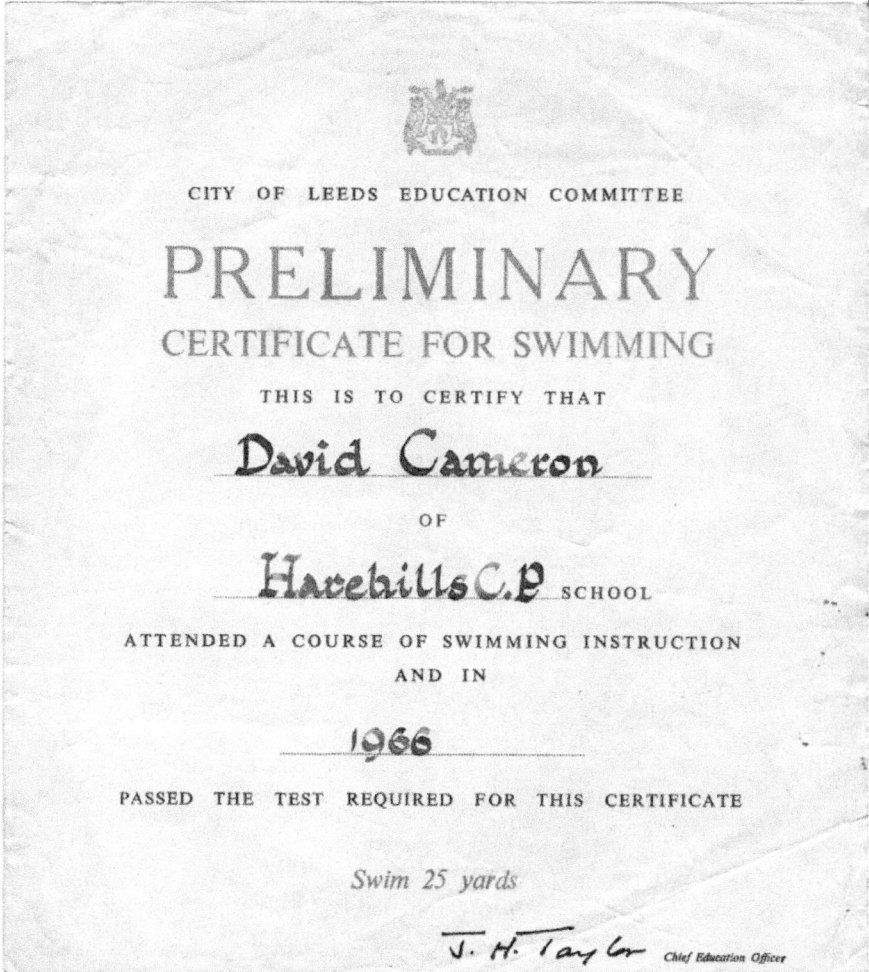

CITY OF LEEDS EDUCATION COMMITTEE

PRELIMINARY

CERTIFICATE FOR SWIMMING

THIS IS TO CERTIFY THAT

David Cameron

OF

Harehills C.P SCHOOL

ATTENDED A COURSE OF SWIMMING INSTRUCTION

AND IN

1966

PASSED THE TEST REQUIRED FOR THIS CERTIFICATE

Swim 25 yards

J. H. Taylor *Chief Education Officer*

humiliation was complete. There was a positive for me, as at least I wasn't the one to feel the heat of shame, wanting the world to swallow you up.

Now some children who had been to baths before knew that there was a possible treat at the end and they had come prepared with some pennies. The baths sold little bags of crackers that looked very much like Ritz crackers. The crackers were very salty and in great demand. We new-comers had to wait, starving, for the next week to come prepared. Over the weeks, I looked forward to the crackers and later there were other offerings: Bovril drinks were available in plastic cups and even Smiths Crisps with the little blue paper twists of salt. There was only one choice of flavour in those days, with salt or without.

As I have mentioned, I think we changed baths at one time and that was due to repair work or something. We only went once a week for one term and, bit by bit, I gained a little confidence. I have lived in Perth, Western Australia, since 1992 and you can see why Australia has such good swimmers. Children often have pools at home, have lessons every day for two weeks and it is warm so that they go on the bus in their swimmers and go back to school just wrapped in a towel. Even adults will turn up at the sports centres in their bathers and leave the same way. So very different from the freezing delights of Leeds in the 1950s!

WINTER AND SCHOOL CHRISTMAS PARTIES

The windup to the end of term and the Christmas holidays was always something that I enjoyed and looked forward to. The teachers always seemed harassed, but cheered up in the last few days and it was only when I became a teacher that I understood why. The weather was miserable and we left home for school in the dark and it was darkening as we made our way home. Often, it was wet and we would have to spend lunch and break times stuck in the class. At these times, the classrooms were extremely noisy and even though teachers patrolled the rooms, the atmosphere and noise was enough to fray the nerves of even the most patient teachers, and Mr. Kelly had a pretty short fuse at the best of times.

Due to these and other factors, I am sure that the end of term couldn't have come soon enough for the staff. We usually had art and craft work that we were getting ready for Christmas and these would include a Christmas card and, most years, a candle ornament for the table. These usually involved holly, pinecones, ribbon, glitter and plaster of Paris. You had to go in search of holly and cones and this involved a trip to Hetchell Woods near Bardsey, where there was always a good supply of holly with berries. As I have mentioned in a previous memory, I wonder how many houses were burnt to the ground as a result of school made gifts. Towards the end of term, carols would be sung in assemblies and there was a real anticipation of something special coming. Who could forget, '*Good King Wenceless Last Looked Out, or While Shepherds Washed their Socks that Night, All*

Seated Round the Tub, the Angel of the Lord Came Down and Showed them How to Scrub, and We three Kings of Orient Tar, Selling Soap at Tuppence a Bar, Chewing Gum Seven Pence, Toffee Eleven Pence, that's all the Prices Are!

Oh, the innocence of the times and the lack of teaching what the correct lyrics were! As we got older the words became less innocent.

My mother as a young woman.

The fog was beginning to become less likely, and there was frost and the possibility of snow. The classrooms began to have a special atmosphere as winter set in, due to rows of wet socks, gloves, hats and scarves drying on the hot heating pipes that edged the classroom. The air could be pungent and steamed up the very tall windows along the outside wall of the room. When the teachers, in our case Mr. Kelly, could stand it no longer, out would come the long window pole and the top window-catches would be hooked and tugged with quite a force to make them open. When we returned to the classrooms after lunch and breaks in the yard, our hands and feet would be frozen. Those, like me, who had holes in the soles of our shoes from playing soccer and from sliding on the frozen tarmac playground, suffered at these times. I learnt very quickly that frozen hands and feet should not be placed on the hot pipes. It was not that the pipes were extremely hot, but rather that the nerves in the hands and feet were numb from the cold and the sudden shock would result in over excited nerves that were excruciatingly painful. Usually, the pipes failed to dry socks and gloves between breaks and lunch, but rather just heated them up. It was a more pleasant experience slipping warm, if wet, gloves and socks onto our feet and hands, but pushing feet then into wet shoes was not enjoyable. If it was thick snow, then we would probably have wellies, but we avoided them otherwise, as they prevented you playing soccer. My gloves were hand-knitted, as were my scarves and hat, but the luckier children might have leather gloves. These were what every boy wanted, as you could make great snowballs without them sticking in little pieces to the wool.

Apart from the cards and candles, we were occupied by getting us to make paper chains and streamers. The chains were made from squares of coloured gummed paper. We would cut strips, ruler width, and then form loops and link the next one through the first loop. A quick lick of the unpleasantly tasting gum, and we hoped they would stick. You had to hold them together for quite a while. Mr. Kelly must have loved it as it took hours to make even a short length of chain. When we had sufficient, we would join them up to others and Mr. Kelly would then hang them around the room from the top of the tall step-ladders. Sometimes, we cut strips from rolls of crepe paper and joined them up with sellotape and twisted them to make streamers. We loved it. It was so much more fun than the usual lessons and we were allowed to talk as we worked. Other decorations would also appear and these opened out from flat shapes to make honeycombed paper bells. The colour had faded a bit over the years they had been used and then stored again, but there was something special about them.

On one of the days before the end of term, we would have our Christmas school dinner. I don't think we knew until we arrived in the hall beneath the church, but the sight of the dinner ladies wearing party hats was always a giveaway. Dinner was sliced turkey, roast potatoes, parsnips, sprouts, stuffing and gravy. It was great, apart from the parsnips and the sprouts, but I now like sprouts. The teachers and dinner ladies were quite jolly and the pudding was Christmas pudding with custard, but it may have had just a taste of brandy in it. I believe that there were threepenny bits in foil inside some, but that might just be my wishful thinking. Nowadays, health and safety would not allow such foolishness, but when I was a teacher at a school near Wakefield I know that there were.

The other event in the final week was the class Christmas party. There was a lot of excitement on the morning and we all came to school with our donation to the feast we were to have. In came a wide range of potted meat sandwiches, sausage rolls, luncheon meat sandwiches, iced buns, butterfly buns, jelly, trifle, cake, egg sandwiches and all manner of culinary creations. Hundreds and thousands and those little silver balls often decorated the icing and there were paper plates and paper bowls for the cake and desserts. The desks were all pushed back around the room and unprinted newspaper was used to cover them. We placed our offerings, hoped they were good enough, and went to inspect what else was on offer. My mother was never a great cook and so I think I always brought sandwiches, but some produced quite impressive cakes. Mr. Kelly had a record player in the room and the chairs were edging the three sides away from the desks with the food and cordial. I thought the room looked smashing, with the streamers, chains and other decorations. I don't remember there ever being a tree, but maybe there was one in the hall. I don't know what Mr. Kelly did to occupy us all in the morning, but maybe we went into the hall, had an assembly and maybe sang carols for a while to keep us all out of mischief. I think we may have had a general knowledge quiz to help pass the time.

Finally, the party started and we didn't have a disco in those days, but we did play games. I remember musical statues, where when the music stopped you had to remain motionless. Mr. Kelly would decide who was the last to stop and they had to sit down. Eventually, there were just two left and there was great competition to be the winner. Another game was musical chairs and we had to bring our chairs out and sit facing away from the next person in a line. The music would start and we had to march around the chairs, waiting for the music to stop. Mr. Kelly removed one of the chairs and when the music stopped, we scrambled to find a chair to sit on. One was unlucky and they had to sit out. This continued and could become quite aggressive, as children almost fought for a seat. You were not allowed to cut through the line and, once again, it got down to just two people. This was fairly serious now and there was great kudos to winning a game. The music seemed to go on for ever, but finally the needle was lifted off the old record player and there was a scramble. The winner was heralded, but I don't remember prizes. I am sure that there must have been other games, but at some point we were allowed to eat. You were told in no uncertain terms not to be greedy and if you took it, you had to eat it. After a while, we were allowed to go back for seconds or to start the desserts. Following this, we played some more games, but I am not sure what. Finally, the end of day came along. We had to help clear up, get rid of the rubbish and make sure we collected plates etc. that came from our homes. I am sure Mr. Kelly must have sighed with relief as we all traipsed out and the room became silent. He must have beaten a hasty retreat to the staff room and had a relaxing cigarette.

The next day was spent cleaning up and taking down streamers etc. I think we must have had a lot of silent reading to keep a lid on the excitement. I do remember one year a message coming to the room and we all had to go down to the gym for Christmas Carols. We all got down, sat in our appropriate lines and Mr. Wilson, the headmaster, came in. I think it was his idea of a joke as he sat down and read the book A Christmas Carol to us. This was the last afternoon and I think he was being kind to the teachers. We sat and listened and I really enjoyed it. I loved listening to stories and this must have been a children's version. What more could a boy or girl want than ghosts, death and a happy ending? Merry Christmas to you all. Bah! Humbug!

SCHOOL TRIPS

I don't think that schoolchildren in the 1950s and 60s went on the number of school visits that they do nowadays and when we did go they were quite memorable occasions. I can only remember two days out at Harehills and one evening visit.

The first day trip was in Year Three with Mr. Kelly to York, but it could have been the Fountains Abbey one that was first, I can't be sure. I think we had to bring in some money to pay for the trip, but I don't think it was very expensive and I don't remember any one of us not being able to go. On the day of the trip, I arrived at school with a paper bag with my lunch in it. As was common at the time, it was a round of sandwiches with potted meat in them and, apart from some butter, there was nothing else. The meat pastes used to come in little glass jars and Shippam's and Prince's were the common ones. There was a range of pastes: salmon, shrimp, potted beef and the one that you were never very sure what was in it, potted meat. The sandwiches were wrapped in grease-proof paper, and there might have been a packet of crisps and an apple. We were all excited and chattered loudly as we piled onto the bus. This wasn't the usual double-decker that we were used to, but was a Wallace Arnold coach. We settled in our seats, next to our friends, and we were given strict instructions that we weren't to eat anything on the coach and we were to wait until it was lunch time. With the final words warning us to keep the noise down, we set off to York.

In these times, the road to York was only a fairly minor one and there wasn't the fast dual-carriageway that exists now. Even so, the journey wasn't a long one and before we knew it we were approaching the city. I had driven through with my parents on the way to the coast on many occasions and I remembered well the beautiful daffodils on the grass banks by the walls, the bright yellow and green being a wonderful contrast, but we had never visited as a family. The coach took us to a place it could park and we piled out and lined up in twos. We had caught glimpses of the city walls and I was captivated by the real history. Knights in armour had walked these walls and now I was going to tread where they had. I believe that we had approached through Bishop's Gate and we went into St George's Field and took a short walk along the medieval walls. From there, I think we walked to the Minster, did a quick tour and then down the Shambles to the Castle Museum. I loved Clifford's Tower, but didn't know of its dark history and then we went into the museum. At first, I hated it and thought it was very boring. Just display after display of costumes, but then we entered the recreated streets with the shops and that was fantastic, just like stepping back into a Dickensian novel. I thought it was wonderful, but then we left, passed the old flour mill and made our way back to where the coach was. We sat near the river to have our lunch. Potted meat sandwiches never tasted so good, and then we all piled onto a boat for a trip down the river past Rowntree's and the Bishop's Palace.

We were fairly exhausted when we arrived back, but we were allowed into a shop selling souvenirs of York and there I made a bold choice. Most of the others were buying postcards, thimbles or other such knick-knacks, but my eye was caught by a sheath knife. It had a four-inch blade and a white enamel handle with the crest of York City. I had enough money, but dare I buy it? What would Mr Kelly say if he saw it? I think it was another classmate that was with me, maybe Dick or Paul, and we both bought one. It was in a brown paper bag and we slipped them out of sight and got back on the bus. We daren't take them out, but had the odd feel just to prove that we had done it. The next problem was what our parents would say. Would they be angry? Would they take them off us? The truth was, they just gave them a cursory glance and said to be careful with them.

Fountains Abbey was a longer journey, but equally fantastic. A Cistercian monastery set in an idyllic rural landscape, it is the largest monastic ruin in England. We arrived and wandered the ruins and got a sense of how magnificent the abbey would have been. I learnt there had been an infirmary and a fish farm at one time. We then walked through the grounds to Studley Royal Water Gardens, built in the 18th century. Truly wonderful, but not as exciting for primary school children, as the ruins. We were once again exhausted on the way home.

Probably the most exciting of all the visits was the evening visit to Civic Theatre. This was my first visit ever to a theatre and probably was for most of us. We were going to see a pantomime, Peter Pan, and we met at school early evening in winter. It was already dark and we piled into the bus that was taking us, and after a short drive into the city, we got out and entered the theatre. As theatres go, it possibly wasn't the most magnificent, but for me it was a wondrous world. Inside were rows of seats, rising up, a stage, lights, big red curtains and a set that had a tree-house and at times turned into a ship, what a world for a young audience! The lights went down in the theatre and the lights came on on the stage, and for the next hour and a half I was swept away. There was Captain Hook, and Peter Pan actually flew across the stage on wires and the cast encouraged the audience to join in and shout back. "He's behind you! Oh no, he's not!" echoed around. We were expected to boo every time the villain appeared. We almost cried when Tinkerbell was fading if we didn't believe in fairies and we all let the cast know we truly believed. How we loved it when she recovered and finally the crocodile was going to get Captain Hook! It was madness, and truly wonderful. I think we were all hoarse afterwards. Up to this point, my experience of anything theatrical was my mother's Christmas sketches that she wrote and everyone at the parties took a part. They were great fun, but this was something else, and I think it was the start of my love of live performances. I don't think we ever did anything quite as exciting at Harehills CP School and it was the first step in starting me writing pantomimes and plays for the schools I worked in for almost forty years.

At Roundhay, I can only remember two cultural visits and one of those was organised by Mr Goldthorpe to the Mikado at, I believe, the Alhambra Theatre. It was an enjoyable event, but seeing as I didn't understand the satire of the piece, I found it just a colourful show with some memorable songs. The second event was a matinee of Julius Caesar, again in Bradford, and this was in the round and was set in Fascist Germany, with storm troopers, machine gun wielding actors, appearing through the audience. This did help to make Shakespeare more relevant to a young audience and was quite an event with machine gun fire during the performance. I have just had a flashback and also remember going to Stratford in the Sixth Form to see King Lear. It was probably a joint excursion with Roundhay Girls' School. The Royal Shakespeare Company production was a modern, 1970s version, and for some reason all the actors were dressed in white. This made it almost impossible to recognise who was who and added nothing to the production. I have a feeling Trevor Nunn might have been responsible. As usual in Shakespeare's plays, I think I was well asleep by the second act.

As adults, we often don't realise the impact the experiences we provide children with have on them. For good or bad, there are teachers I remember so well. Some were very unpleasant people, but most were very well-intentioned and some I loved. I really liked my teachers, and my time at Stainbeck Preparatory School and Harehills. At Roundhay, I had good and bad experiences, but often I didn't help myself and I can see why I would irritate some teachers. I don't think I would have spent my life in education if my own experiences hadn't been so positive. I am aware of at least one of my students who ended up as a professional actor and I would like to think that the experiences they had in my schools helped to foster a wide range of careers.

CAPTIVE IN THE CASTLE.

It started with my brother, but then was passed down to me, and that was the annual Easter visit to my aunty and uncle's house. Initially, they lived in Coventry and I remember both of the houses they owned with fond memories. Grandma and Grandad, Mary and Harry, would take the bus to Coventry and there be met by my aunty and uncle. Andrew went for a number of years and I was quite envious of the two or three days' adventure. I had to wait until I was about ten or eleven, before it became my turn. My brother was about thirteen or fourteen and he would have thought himself too grown up, so I was invited.

I am not sure what the reason was: anxiety, a bad experience or just keen, but the journey always started at the crack of dawn. We would catch the double-decker bus to Leeds City and there go to the Wellington Street bus station. Now we would arrive, probably at 8.30am and the bus did not leave until about 11.00am. It was so early that the sign for the Coventry bus was not yet on display and we would stand for ages before the sign would eventually be placed on a stand and we knew where we should wait. And wait we did! The initial excitement became utter boredom. There was nothing to do, or at least nothing that we were going to do, but stand and wait. Just before I was about to die, the bus turned up. We got on, found our places and it was still a long wait before anyone else even turned up to board. The bus was not an express and it stopped at six towns along the route. What could have been not much more than a two and a half hour journey was six hours on this bus. It was absolute hell

148

for me and I can't think great fun for my grandparents, dealing with a restless child for that length of time. There are only so many things your eye can spy on the route and only so many minutes a comic: Beano, Dandy or Topper, can last. Once you have seen Chesterfield's crooked spire, you have seen it, and with breathing in diesel fumes, lead pollution and smoke from the rear of the single-decker coach I can't say I felt too well. The regular sweets and toffees helped a little, but if there is purgatory, then this bus route is it. Sisyphus would

Kenilworth trip - Me, cousin Angela, Aunty Joan, Grandma and Grandad.

have enjoyed pushing the boulder up the hill as a bit of light relief in comparison.

Eventually, towards the end of the day, we would arrive and after the obligatory hugs and kisses we would be in the car to my aunt and uncle's house. At first, it was in Coventry and they had what seemed to me to be a lovely new semi-detached house on a new estate. They moved to Kenilworth after one or two future trips and Kenilworth was beautiful. Brookside Avenue was, again, a new development around a small village of thatched cottages, pubs and small stores, in the shadow of a magnificent castle. Kenilworth was now a small town and it was a feeder for the major cities of Coventry and Birmingham.

What more could a young boy want than a castle? It didn't matter that it was ruined, blown up during the English Civil War, and maybe that made it even more exciting. It was once a magnificent building, greatly extended since its Norman origins to the scene of Earl of Leicester's grand hosting of Elizabeth I's court in 1575. The queen was canny enough to deal with any perceived threat by her lords, either due to popularity or wealth, by visiting with her court. In this case, there was the addition of romance and the Earl spent a vast amount on entertaining Her Majesty for three weeks. At one point, the water meadow was flooded so that mock naval battles could take place and there were water-borne fireworks from papier-mâché dolphins.

My aunty, cousin and I went to visit the castle. I was excited. Its massive fortifications were and still are very impressive. Most of the structure is in a state of ruin, but there was sufficient for me to get a sense of what it would have been like and to ponder who else had trodden the same steps, centuries earlier. I was in heaven, and the bus trip was very soon forgotten. I am not sure if it is still the case, but you were allowed to scale the keep, and the steps led to windows that overlooked the grounds and gave magnificent views of the wonderfully lush countryside. My cousin was a couple of years younger than me, but she appeared to have absolutely no fear of heights. I have always had a realistic sense of my own vulnerability and as a result, been safety conscious. I must admit, some of my close calls have not obviously demonstrated this. A single metal bar would separate the observer from a fall that would certainly have proven fatal, but yet my cousin would lean right over the edge as if tempting the fates to do their worst. I could barely stand to watch her, but my aunty seemed to share her lack of concern.

We had arrived in the afternoon and were enjoying the late sunshine, the crowds had thinned and we were busy exploring. There was some sort of distant siren, but we paid it no heed. Maybe half an hour later, we were starting to get tired and hungry and my aunty led us back to the gate we had entered. We did notice that there didn't seem anyone around, but it was only when we got to the gate and saw that it was closed and locked, did it dawn on us that the siren was the signal the castle was closing for the day, and now it was closed and everyone had left. Castles are designed to keep people out, but they work just as well keeping people in. I think I saw my aunty panic for the first time. There truly was no one there and it was starting to get dark. My goat-like cousin saved the day by scaling the wall near the gate and climbing down. I had no problem following suit, but I think my aunt struggled a bit. The alternative of spending the night alone in the castle, or suffering the embarrassment and indignity of the authorities being contacted to let her out, provided sufficient incentive and she followed suit. Once out, we had a bit of a laugh about it and made a note to check closing times in the future.

SHORT BACK AND SIDES

Another lasting memory from primary school days was having my hair cut. My mother would regularly give me money and tell me to get my hair cut on the way home after school. On the other side of the road from Harehills C.P. school, there were a couple of barbers' shops, I seem to remember, and there was a definite atmosphere about them. As you entered, you were hit by the smell of Brylcreem and aftershave. There were chairs in front of the window where you waited in turn and the linoleum floor had a carpet of hair, that was occasionally swept. If there were men in the shop, the air would have the additional aroma of smoke. Whilst waiting, you would look at the magazines and sometimes find some racy pictures to keep you occupied. The shelves were supplied with all sorts of things for sale that I had no idea about. What were styptic pencils, condoms and why would I want Wilkinson Sword safety razors? It was all an adult male mystery to me.

I used to watch the barber in action. Hair was combed, raised between two fingers, and trimmed with a sharp pair of scissors. This process was continuous and the fingers were a blur. Somehow, in just a few minutes, an unruly mop of hair would become a well-managed work of art. Water was sprayed from a bottle, a cut-throat razor would appear, sharpened on a leather belt, and the back of the neck would be expertly shaped and cleared of unwanted hair. A few wafts of a soft brush, a flick of the wrist and any cut hair was removed. A mirror was held up, approval sought and then the covering sheet, protecting the customer, was whisked off like a matador at a bull fight. Money was exchanged and then the barber would turn around and say, 'Next?"

If I was next, then a plank of wood was laid over the two arms of the chair so that the smaller customers were at a height that meant the barber didn't have to bend. "What will it be?". To this there didn't seem a lot of choice, it was usually short back and sides, or short back and sides with a square neck. I did once try a crew cut, but with my fine hair it wouldn't stand up like my brother's. Anyway, the magic of the comb and scissors was utilised and then the clippers came out. I believe it had the subtlety of a New South Wales sheep shearer, but within a few moments, a mirror was held up for approval. I have no idea what would have happened if I had said I wasn't happy with something and I wasn't game to find out. He would ask if you wanted lacquer and if you said 'yes', you were sprayed with some highly scented liquid that set with a crusty finish to your hair. Out came the brush, two swift flicks or so and then the apron was unfastened, additional swishes to ensure some hair went down the back of the neck to itch for an eternity and then a hand was stretched out to receive payment.

I would leave the shop a squirming mess, but look in the nearby shop window reflection to see what sort of fashion statement I made. My mother would check to see that I had been shorn as I entered through our door and nod her approval, whilst I would still be unable to stop gyrating and removed my shirt, shook it vigorously to remove any remnants of the hair. Now, I would be grateful to have that hair back, but such is the experience of youth that we don't appreciate what we have until it is gone.

FINAL YEARS

After my mother got over the delight of my going to Roundhay School, there was a hiatus where life returned to normality and Mr Kelly, at Harehills County Primary, continued in his usual form. When he became frustrated, out came his, 'Angels and Ministers of Grace Defend Us!', call to divine intervention to help the children under his charge. Funnily, that was as aggressive as I remember him being, but I believe that he was prone to using corporal punishment with the slipper. I do remember some of us questioning him once about why he had brown stains on his fingers and he told us that it was from peeling a lot of apples. Even in our innocence, we didn't believe that one.

The rest of the year seemed more relaxed and we saw the introduction of ballpoint pens and the removal of the dip pens, blotting paper and inkwells. There was some excitement at having the coloured pens, shaped very much like an ink pen, stubby at the point and tapering to a thin end. The ritual filling of inkwells, asking for blotting paper and occasional replacement nibs, disappeared overnight. I missed the ability to flick pellets of ink-soaked blotting paper at girls sitting in the rows in front and using the pens as darts and throwing them into the bare floorboards, where a good shot would have it stuck in the wood, swaying from side to side. Of course, that would never be done when Mr Kelly was in the room.

Times were very different in 1960s and along with the disappearance of the ink pens a whole new world was opening up. Cliff Richard had appeared in the film, Summer Holiday, in 1963 which starts in black and white, but once the bus reaches Europe it changes to full colour. It was another film I saw with my grandma in the Dominion in Chapel Allerton. The change of colour in the film is like the change that occurred in my life at this time. The old was black and white and the new was bright and colourful. The pens were vivid red, bright green or yellow and the new desks that arrived weren't double desks with iron frames. There was a general sense of optimism that hadn't been there before. There was to be a brave new world and we were to experience it head-on. I even remember one Friday afternoon, a man and woman arriving at the classroom and they wanted our opinions on a number of chocolate bars. Now I am sure this wouldn't be permissible nowadays, but for some reason it was ok then. The bars were all unwrapped and we were given no indication what any of them were called. We were handed some to try and we had to give them scores for our preferences. One was very much like a Milky Way and another like a Mars Bar. It is possible it was the prototype Aztec Bar that was Cadbury's answer to the Mars Bar. The Aztec was launched for the Mexico Olympics in 1968 so it is possible. Anyway, that was a memorable day, but unfortunately one that was never repeated.

As summer approached, the school selected a cricket team. Now I don't remember many opportunities for inter-school sports, but I think a new keen male teacher organised one. We had trials and some practices on a Saturday morning on the Soldiers' Field at Oakwood. We weren't up to much and the equipment was basic. The pads were old, torn and heavy, and we found them difficult to run in, but wearing them made you feel special. The bats were old, fairly battered and smelt of linseed oil. I loved the smell and, just writing this, the odour is filling my mind. We used to play cricket at lunch and break times on the tarmac yard at Harehills, using tennis balls, with wickets that were painted on the caretaker's house wall. There was a slope down to the wicket and some kids could build up a real pace. I was just ok at batting and bowling and I turned up for the selection practice, which I seem to remember happened after school in the yard. Joy above joy, I was selected and turned up on Saturday for a proper practice with anticipation and pride! I batted and scored about seven runs, which I was quite pleased with. I think we were limited to only batting a couple of overs. The first game with another school came along and I have no idea if we won, but I scored twelve runs, so I was delighted. I think we only had one or two more matches, but I do remember my dad turning up to watch one that was after school. I think it was somewhere near Crossgates and this was on a proper cricket pitch. The time came for me to bat and I strode out, knowing that my dad was watching. I was nervous, but it was one of those days where everything worked out. I seemed to see the ball more easily and I scored twenty, with one four. I was over the moon and my dad seemed quite impressed. I went home with him in his car rather than on the bus and I think it was the only time he ever saw me play in a match. It still means a lot.

Boys wore shorts at primary school and, in fact, well into high school. I was no exception, and I had a rather baggy pair of grey school shorts. We didn't have many clothes and we wore them until they became threadbare and patched. I often remember hand-me-downs from my brother or neighbours. Washing was something that was done once a week and not daily, as is now the case. I think I used to wear my school shirt all week. Anyway, I didn't own a pair of long trousers at the time and this was to prove interesting. My mother received some complimentary tickets for the Silver Blades ice skating rink on Kirkstall Road, near the Yorkshire Television buildings. Now, my mother could have won them. She was keen on entering competitions and she was quite successful. Never having been ice skating, it was an exciting opportunity and my mum, my brother and I were dropped off by Dad and we went in and exchanged our shoes for some very uncomfortable ice skating boots.

They laced up to above the ankle and the rink was a hive of activity. The cold hit you and the air had a vibrancy that gave sounds a higher tone that shocked the senses. It was nigh on impossible to walk in the skates. My legs splayed out like a baby giraffe taking its first steps. I staggered to the nearest entrance onto the ice, and holding onto the rail, stepped out. Now the rink was full of capable skaters of all ages. They flashed by with unimaginable ease and grace. There were those who showed off by skating backwards, dodging between the laggards, impressing everyone and particular the opposite sex. It was just like the men on the waltzers at the fairground. Music blared, and in the centre of the revolving masses a girl, clearly a figure skater, demonstrated what we could all aspire to. I wanted to be like them. How hard could it be? It was at this point that I felt the cold air around my knees and then the horror struck me. I was the only boy in the place in short trousers. Everyone else was suitably attired in long trousers, even many of the girls. The horror of my faux pas hit me and a sudden rush of heat spread all over me, sending the chill well into retreat. I looked at my mum. How could she have done this to me? Of course she was oblivious. I stood there, horrified, but as I had no option, I stepped off from the edge and attempted to emulate all the others around. I did notice that many of them were very shaky and collisions and falls were common. Surely it couldn't be that hard, I thought, and I set off. One push off, a wobble and then disaster. The ice was hard, cold and wet and I was splayed on my back like an overturned beetle. Getting back on my feet was easier said than done and a very ungracious crawl to the side followed. I pulled myself up and noticed that my brother seemed to be mastering the skill, even in a very basic way. I tried again and, bit by bit, I managed to get a balance and pushed and pulled myself around the edge. Finally I took courage to let go of the side and pushed off. I was skating! I shuffled myself along, and over time, grew in confidence and built up the speed. The problem was that no one had told me how to stop or turn. I went in a straight line across the rink, others almost diving aside to avoid me and I shot at speed, pink-kneed, pink-faced and out of control, until I went smack into the opposite side and hit the ice again. Having gained some confidence, I continued on, noting that my brother was annoyingly smooth and controlled. After half an hour or so, I reached the stage of managing a circuit. My turns, though far from elegant, were beginning to be effective, and with pressure being exerted to the outer foot I could gain directional control.

There was a master of ceremonies, or disc jockey for those old enough to know what a disc is, and at times he would clear the ice for speed skating or for the machine to go out and groom the ice. This was the time I sat with my brother and mum and had a drink. After the break, I and my embarrassing pink and almost bleeding knees ventured back out. It was a bit easier this time and I felt better, until a girl fell in front of me and I had neither the ability nor the knowledge of how to stop in time or swerve to avoid her. I hit her side-on and flew like a graceless dodo and landed face forward into the ice, spread-eagled like a star. This fallen star had had enough by now. The girl was getting up and so I knew I hadn't cut her in half, like the lady in a box with a magician. The blades for beginners were fairly blunt, but I did wonder if they could cut a finger if one was skated over. I managed to get back to my feet and continued, more because I felt I had to and I didn't want to be beaten by anything. At this point in my life, I had managed to succeed to a reasonable level in everything I had done, so I wasn't going to be defeated by this. Soon mum was indicating our time was up. We went around one more time and then managed to make the right exit, even if too fast, and smashed into the side wall. Out of breath, out of patience and knees out in the open, I was glad to get the skates off and return them and get my wonderfully comfortable shoes back. Dad was waiting as arranged, and on the way home even my mum agreed I needed some long trousers.

This wasn't my only attempt at it as we did go back at least a couple more times. The next occasion was more successful and my knees didn't get another outing. Looking back, I am not sure if this wasn't the first time that I had experienced real embarrassment and a sense of lack of control. There are many times since that I have experienced both, but at eleven years old I suppose your development gives you a greater anxiety regarding how you are perceived. Of course, at my current age, I have lost many of my inhibitions and often delight in being embarrassing, much to the horror of my children and long-suffering wife!

CUBS AND SCOUTS

It was my elder brother who was the trailblazer for me as I grew up. He was the first to try everything, being four years older than me, and so it was with the cubs. He attended Ladywood Methodist Church pack and he seemed to have a good time. It was always something that I assumed I would do when I was old enough, but as it turned out, it was not to be. I was quite envious, as he wore a green jumper, neckerchief and woggle. I think they also had a cap in those days, but I am not sure.

Whilst the family attended Ladywood, my parents got quite involved. My mother did keep fit there and somehow my father got roped in to running the soccer team for the cubs. The good news was that my brother would always make the team and the bad news, it meant dad had to organise practices and attend matches. As my dad and brother were going, I also had to attend, but couldn't participate in any matches. I don't remember minding and the practices used to take place on the Soldiers' Field between Oakwood and Roundhay. Soccer boots in those days were a bit of a joke, and thinking back it was probably due to the cubs that my brother and I got boots and a soccer ball as a Christmas present. The boots were heavy leather with leather studs nailed into the soles and they had a big round toecap that made it difficult to control the ball. In the late 1950s, even professional soccer players were handicapped by their equipment. Shorts were long and of thick cotton, shirts similarly heavy-duty with long sleeves and collars and their boots very big and cumbersome. The soccer balls were terribly heavy leather with laces where the bladder fitted. They hurt when you kicked them and soaked up any water and became impossible to kick more than a few yards. But the worst thing was if you foolishly headed a wet ball. The consequence of a header, if you remained conscious, was probable concussion and long-term brain damage. It was a truly horrendous experience and a mistake I only ever made once or twice.

At the practices, I was occasionally allowed to take part, but I can't say that I was any kind of potential Stanley Matthews. I remember attending a few soccer matches and we would go along and support the team from the sidelines. I think pieces of oranges were provided for the players at half-time. There was one particular Saturday morning when the match was away at Crossgates. My dad took my brother and me in the car, and our pet poodle, Sabot, was taken along at the request of my mother. I suppose it gave her some time to herself with my younger brother, without the rest of us being there. We were living in Gipton Wood Crescent at this time and Crossgates was quite a distance away. The game was not particularly eventful for me, but my brother may have had a different take on it. I have no idea who won, but at the end, my dad bundled the two of us back in the car and we set off for home. We arrived tired, but happy and it was only after a few minutes that Mum asked where Sabot was. Now, this was not a good question for my father as he had let the dog off for a while when the game was going and he had forgotten all about Sabot when organising for the team to be picked up by parents, and getting us into the car. We had left the dog behind. My mum went mad, as only she could, and the blame was directed at my father with passion. I believe that she would have preferred it if he had left one of us behind, rather than the dog.

We were immediately sent back, with the mission of finding Sabot and the inference not to return without him. My poor dad was really in the doghouse. His whole demeanour drooped and any support from my brother or me was met with a tirade from my mum. It was with some relief that we got back in the car, no seat belts in these days, and retraced our steps. The park was deserted when we returned and our hearts sank when there was no sign of Sabot. We called and wandered the area, but it was no use. Dad got us back in the car and we drove the streets of the area, with the forlorn hope of finding Sabot. He did have a collar with our address on it and we hoped that if we didn't find him, someone else would and they would contact us.

Eventually, we had to head home sans dog. My mother's mood had if anything darkened and you could cut the atmosphere with a knife, and if one had been lying around, I wouldn't have fancied my father's chances. Saturday afternoon passed slowly and my mum took to wandering the streets, searching and calling for the dog. My father tried again and set off to look for it. I don't think he would have dared stay at home. But all to no avail. My mother was forlorn and desperate and her heart was truly broken. I had never seen her so upset. It was her dog and her husband and her sons had let her down. The evening was just setting in and all hope had been abandoned and probably divorce was on the cards, when there was a scratching on the door. We all leapt to our feet and mum was the fastest. She opened the door and there was a rather tired and wet looking Sabot. The not overly-endowed with intelligence poodle had somehow managed to find its way home. This was truly amazing, as it had been taken in the car and it wouldn't have seen the route through the window as it sat on the back seat, but somehow, and we will never know how, it had found its way home.

My mother was in heaven. The thing was hugged to within an inch of its life. Fresh lamb's heart was boiled on the stove and it was fed tasty morsels to build back its energy. I am sure it gave my father a look as if to say, "That'll teach you to leave me behind! I hope you suffered!" As it was, family life returned to normal. My father got some colour back in his ashen face and he refrained from comment, content that there was some hope of a future for him. Anything he might have said would not have been well received, after he had left Sabot, mum's most precious possession, behind.

In time, things did settle down and dad continued to take the cub's soccer for the rest of the season, but we never left Sabot behind again. In fact, I can't remember Sabot attending another match. The miracle of his return became just another legend of the family, fading over time.

I never got to attend cubs as we stopped going to Ladywood before I was old enough, but I did go to Scouts. My elder brother was friends with David Musgrove who lived on Easterly Road and we used to play Risk with his younger brother, Richard. There was a even younger brother known as Titch, but like my younger brother, he was too young to be included. Richard attended St. Stephen's Church Scouts on Cramner Road in Moor Allerton and he asked if I would like to join. After discussion with my parents and an understanding that my father didn't want to become involved, I was allowed to go. Richard and I went by bus and the first time I was a little nervous. Now, from what I remember about St. Stephen's Church, it was quite modern in those days (mid 1960s). The design was functional and the altar section of the church had a dividing wall that could be closed and the area where the congregation would sit became the hall when the chairs were stacked and moved back. I was introduced to the leaders and I was allocated a pack and I lined up with them. They were all in uniform, but I was in civvies. There was the usual Scout chant and procedures and then we split up to practise various skills towards badges. I think I was put in the knot-tying group and we had diagrams that showed how to tie bowlines, sheep shanks, clover hitches, reef knots and granny knots and various others. The night passed quickly and ended with games and then we helped pack away and I was invited back the next week. We were told we would be playing 'wide games', so not to come in uniform. I had no idea what that meant, but Richard told me we would be in the woods and to come in clothes that wouldn't get spoiled.

The next week came and we arrived at St. Stephen's. After the initial rituals, we were led down to the woods and there we were told the rules. There were two teams. One team was defending the base and they would patrol and search for any intruders. If you saw someone and called out their name, they had to surrender and were held captive in the base. The attacking team could free the captives by sneaking into the base and announcing they had done so and then all the captives could escape. There wasn't really a winner, but if you captured all the attackers, then victory would be yours. I don't think I ever played the game where any team won.

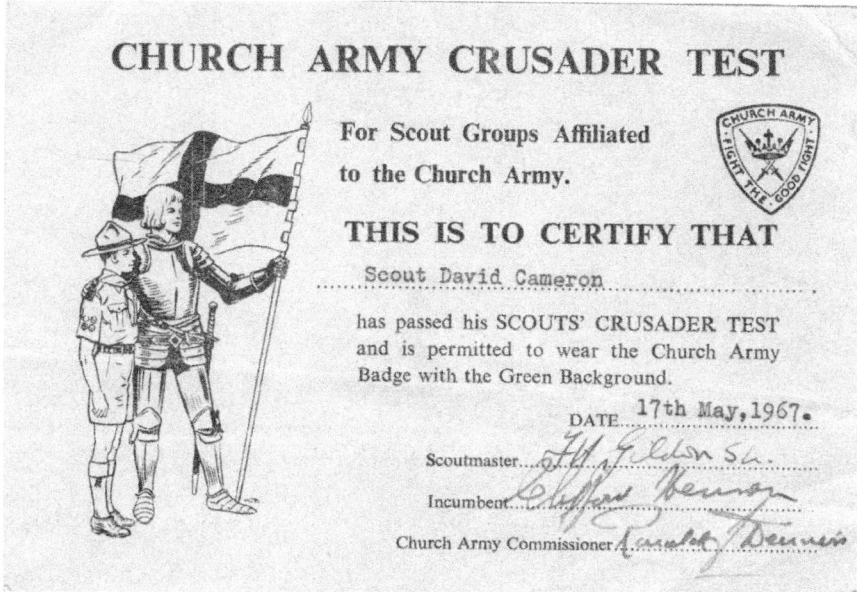

CHURCH ARMY CRUSADER TEST

For Scout Groups Affiliated to the Church Army.

THIS IS TO CERTIFY THAT

Scout David Cameron

has passed his SCOUTS' CRUSADER TEST and is permitted to wear the Church Army Badge with the Green Background.

DATE 17th May, 1967.

Scoutmaster...........................

Incumbent...........................

Church Army Commissioner...........................

I was in the attacking team and we had to sneak up on the defenders. They were not allowed to stay near the base, as that would make the attackers' task impossible. Lying in the long grass and bushes was a dirty and scratchy affair. Grass cuts were common and irritating after the game, but you never noticed during it. I was in my element and any concerns I had about joining the Scouts disappeared that evening. I was ecstatic! It was all a boy could want. I went home that night, tired, filthy and euphoric. Scouting was for me!

WINTER

Before the days of central heating and double glazing, houses really knew when winter had arrived. Temperatures in the bedroom would plummet and the windows would be covered in the silvery ferns of ice. Children nowadays would not know the magic of the iced windows or the joy of scraping a bit clear to gaze out on the white hoar frosted garden, before the image disappeared as the window misted and refroze. At times like these, the covers were heavy on the beds and I used to cover my head to maintain any warmth. I am surprised that we didn't suffocate, but somehow we managed and eventually emerged and dressed as rapidly as possible. Breakfast was often porridge at such times and the warmth, top of the milk and a spoonful of sugar set my brothers and me up for the day.

If it was a school day, then a couple of pairs of socks forced into wellies helped, coat, scarf and knitted gloves, and I was prepared for the outside. Early on such mornings, the world looked magical: my breath of steam would hang on the still air and each breath in would chill all the way to the lungs with air that would often taste of smoke. The garden was bare and the black sticks were covered in a coating of ice. As the watery sun caught the light, the crystals would sparkle and there was a clarity that was breathtaking. The first steps on the white grass left prints that traced our passage and joined those of the early birds, who were struggling to find food. The milk bottles by the back door would have their foil tops pushed off by the frozen milk and would offer no nourishment for the birds. Each step was risky, as the paths and pavements were icy, offering a quick fall to any unwary or careless pedestrian. One of the great joys was standing on the frozen puddles and cracking the thin, unbroken ice. Another was the ability to slide along the pavements, adding to the danger for others following, and wearing holes through the soles of our shoes.

By midday, the ice would just start to melt and then shortly afterwards would refreeze and icicles would form, hanging off the gutters like rows of dagger teeth. If this came after a period of snow, then icicles could grow long and heavy and were a real danger if they snapped and fell. Passing under them was a trial to rival the sword of Damocles. The more wary would hunt out the clothes prop and knock them off before they could create harm. Of course, the re-frozen melt was even slippier and I remember slipping and falling on many occasions. I suppose my bones must have been solid or at least flexible, as I never broke any, but I am sure there would have been many less fortunate who would have a trip to hospital. There was a real pleasure in sucking icicles, but I do remember they did have a sooty flavour, the result of the coal burning fires. On really icy days, Gipton Wood would become a scene of stark beauty, as the bare black tree trunks contrasted with the white covering of frost. The light would barely get above twilight in mid-winter and few people ventured into the wood. Dogs were often just let out the front door and returned of their own free will. Like wolves, they tended to form small packs and sometimes bounded between the trees, enjoying the freedom to roam. Later in the afternoon, on still days, the mist would start to collect and the one light in the wood created a spectral world as it illuminated the vapour like a skirt around its base.

The world changed again when it did snow. Deep snow was not a common event and I can still remember the times when it happened. As a young child, I would open the back door and the snow was above the step and partially blocked the exit. I would step over into a world like no other. The world of snow is a place where sound is altered, muffled and the usual sounds become unfamiliar and intriguing. Steps on dry snow produce a crumping sound and if snow is still falling there is the magic of flakes settling on your nose and face and if you open your mouth wide, onto your tongue. Early in the morning, you were aware of the snow, as the sounds that entered your bedroom were muffled and the light changed to a reflected white without the yellow of sunlight. As you pulled back the curtain and looked out the window, everything had changed. The garden was unrecognisable, with lumps and bumps where familiar landmarks had been. The tree branches bowed under the weight of the gathered snow and were more like white weeping willows. Snow meant a rush to get dressed and be out. There was nothing better than being the first out in it. My brothers and I would get the wooden sledge that our father had made for us out of the garage and we would set off. Like Scott of the Antarctic, we would set out through the virgin snow, one the trail blazer and the others following in the footsteps. The streets were similarly changed: kerbs had disappeared and the pavements led onto the road with no boundaries. Early in the 1960s, there was little traffic and on deep snow days, none at all. We would try making snow balls, but with woollen gloves it was more difficult and if it was very cold, the snow would be too dry to make good ones.

My elder brother was four years my senior and we often headed off to Gipton Wood. There was a reasonable slope that led past the light down to the steps onto Roundhay Road. It was not the best sledging area, but it was local and the best on offer. Sometimes it became quite popular, and by the evening the snow would begin to freeze and form more of an ice sheet that produced an excellent run at high speed. The wooden sledge did not have metal runners and we had to wax them with a big candle. Once waxed, it gave a reasonable run, but the best we had was the old frame off the rocking donkey. The frame was red metal and the stuffed donkey had wheels so that a toddler could be pushed on it. It also had the ability for the handle to fold under and produced a rocking donkey. It wasn't very safe and wouldn't be allowed nowadays, as anything more than a very gentle rock would cause it to overbalance. The donkey had been well-loved by us boys and was getting quite threadbare at this time. I suppose it must have been my brother Andrew's idea, but by removing the donkey, the remaining frame, produced a small, but serviceable sledge. Now, Andrew was quite good at coming up with such ideas and this accompanied by no sense of self preservation, led him to quite a few scrapes. He was, in fact, quite accident-prone as a child, something I took over from as a teenager and beyond. Anyway, I dragged the sledge and he took the donkey frame to Gipton Wood at about six thirty in the evening. It was a startlingly cold night and the snow that had thawed during the day was now frozen solid. It was one of the days when the run down the woods had been well used, but as it was quite dark when we arrived, only one or two keen stragglers were still there and soon they also left. I started to sledge down the slope, using the wooden sledge and enjoyed it, getting a fairly modest speed and a reasonably long run. Andrew used the donkey frame and was staggered by the initial speed he got and he just managed to stop before the wall that fell down onto the old tram track verge below the wall opposite The Gipton pub. As we trudged back up the hill, there was wild chatter as we were getting the best runs we had ever had in the wood. We took turn after turn and every time, Andrew was faster and sledged further, needing to use his heels to stop shooting off over the wall like some young Eddie the Eagle. The temperature at this point was extremely cold and the snow had gone on the run and been replaced by solid ice. This made the climb back up the hill very difficult. There were ridges down the slope and if you got enough speed, the sledge could just leave the ground a little and often produced a spill. When the snow was soft, this just was cause for much laughter and all part of the joy of sledging. We both had a great time and decided that we would have one last go. Andrew was going first and he sat on the small metal donkey frame, pushed off and shot like a bullet down the slope. He must have used extra force as it was his final go, and there was the sound like an ice-skate cutting through the ice as he hit the first ridge. This time he was airborne, and I don't mean slightly. He took to the air like some kind of miniature Santa Claus on his sleigh. Unfortunately, he didn't have the magic power and the sledge was overtaken by gravity and landed with a bang onto solid ice. His balance gone, he slewed sideways, but continued at a great pace. He hit the next ridge sideways on, shot into the air, separated from the donkey frame, there was a swirl of arms and legs and then a sickening crack as his head hit the ice. Luckily, he was wearing the obligatory woolly hat with a pompom, and this must have helped a bit. He lay on the ground, stunned, and not moving a great deal. I rushed down to find him slowly getting to his feet, holding his head in considerable pain. He headed home and I followed, dragging the sledge with the donkey frame sitting on it. I am sure that he was concussed, but at that time and at my age I had no idea what it was. Luckily, the Camerons are nothing if not thick-skulled, and no long term damage resulted, or at least none that was diagnosed.

When I was a little older and there was a good snow fall, we sometimes would head to Roundhay Park. Now, Roundhay Park has a wonderful tiered slope that leads down to the arena called Hill Sixty, named after a site in the First World War, I believe. On the other side, nearer the mansion, there is a smoother, less steep slope that is perfect for sledging. When the conditions were suitable, hundreds would turn up to enjoy the thrill of hurtling down the hill, to be followed by the long trudge back up. By the time you got back up to the top, you were sweating profusely, despite the icy air. I remember the occasional show-off would arrive with skis and show their skills by weaving down the slope. This area was much safer than Gipton Wood, but there was the additional danger of crashes and I do remember quite a few children and adults getting injured.

The other joy of winter at Roundhay Park was when the lakes froze. This didn't happen often, but one year the ice on the little lake was so thick that hundreds of people ventured onto it. Nowadays, I am sure it would not be allowed and it would be policed to make sure no one went onto the ice. I do remember throwing stones across the icy surface and it made a strange skittering noise as it careened across. Some parts the ice were white, but in other thinner parts it was transparent and you could see the world of fish and plants trapped below. The big lake was only once frozen enough to venture on, that I can remember, but often when it was partially frozen, the poor ducks and swans would pad across, looking for a unfrozen section. I always wondered how the poor things coped with the cold conditions.

CHRISTMAS

The memories of my earlier Christmases saw not only changes in the house we lived in, but changes in society and the development of technology. When my brothers and I were little, we were happy that Santa brought us anything. On a number of years, we visited Santa in the big stores in Leeds, probably Lewis'. We were lined up and waited as patiently as young children can near Santa's grotto for our turn to sit on his knee and tell him our deepest wishes. There was the timeless question of whether we had been 'naughty or nice', and then we were given a gift. For a number of years it was the same Blow Football game, which was basically two straws, a small football and a couple of goals. It wasn't much, but it was still a thrill.

The home parties became more elaborate as we got older and I do remember that for my birthday, which is early in December, I got some money and I bought a puppet theatre kit from Varleys' at Harehills' shops. I spent quite a bit of time building the theatre and even added lights using a battery, wires, bulbs and holders. The actors were card figures on a long wire that could be pushed in and out. The stage wasn't very big, maybe 14 inches, but in a small room, with the lights out and with the stage lit, it produced a decent effect. Mum, my brothers and I took the parts and read from a script. I can't for the life of me remember whether the script was written by me or my mum. Anyway, the captive audience was appreciative and, clearly, it must have been fantastic! Well, at least nobody complained. My brothers and my cousin Angela were also roped in to perform at the parties. Anyone with the hint of a talent was brought out, and over the years, recorders, violins, clarinets and guitars made an appearance, usually never to return. Many a carol was sung and now I realise the pleasure that the young are to adults, especially at Christmas.

My father worked at Catton's Steel foundry on Black Bull Street in Hunslet and he became the Chief Inspector of Steel Castings during the 1960s. I would occasionally visit the foundry with my father if he had to go in and check on some work and I remember the smell well. There was a very distinct atmosphere, as liquid steel was poured into the sand moulds. Sparks would fly everywhere and it was exciting and like something out of Dante's Inferno. Of course, children in a foundry wouldn't be allowed nowadays with modern health and safety, but I loved it. Every year the foundry held a Christmas party for the children of the employees. I believe it was on a Saturday afternoon and my big brother and I would be driven to the works. The party was in a large upstairs room with industrial windows down each side. I don't know what it was used for normally, but on these days it was full of scores of children. I am not sure of all things that we did, but I recall we had quite a feast and then they showed films. The projector in those days was very unreliable and I can still hear the cries of anguish from the children as the film snapped at the most dramatic point, or the funniest, if it was a cartoon. At the end of the evening each of the children was given a present from Santa and a tired and excited horde made their way home in either cars or on local buses.

As I got older, Christmas began to evolve. Many of the simple early experiences began to change. The introduction of television was major, but so was the ready supply of compact and portable record players. I do remember that one Christmas my brother received a red Dansette record player. I don't think it was new, but came from a neighbour. However, for a pre-teen boy it was wonderful. Pop music was in its halcyon days: Elvis, Cliff, The Shadows, Billy J Kramer, Adam Faith and many others were coming in and going out of style fairly rapidly. Of course, Cliff Richard is still about, and Elvis never really went out, even after his death, but the biggest rising stars were the Beatles, and 'Please Please Me' was released in 1963. On November 22nd of the same year, the second album, 'With the Beatles' was released, and that was the year my brother got the Dansette and the album. I know that my mother was keen on the Beatles and so she probably was the reason that this album was chosen. It came with some old records and one was by Joseph

Locke. It was a very old rousing song called 'Blaze Away' which my father loved and would sing at the top of his voice. We all hated it! Another record was a Frank Sinatra long player and one of the songs was 'High Hopes - the Rubber Tree Plant song'. The album was called 'All the Way' and was released in 1961. Anyway, the record player was useful for Christmas parties as it allowed better control for Pass the Parcel and other games, though I'm not sure that dropping the very heavy arm onto a new album would have added a great deal to the sound.

I do know that one of the first records my brother bought was 'House of the Rising Sun' by The Animals. The two of us went to Varley's shop at Harehills and bought a copy of the single in June the following year. The Dansette also featured in one of his most disappointing presents a few years later in 1968. He was just beyond a teenager and was into Pink Floyd. The previous year he had bought a copy of The Piper at the Gates of Dawn, which I still have the same copy of. He saw himself as quite hip and trendy and you can imagine his reaction when our lovely grandma from Chapel Allerton gave him a present. He opened it in front of everyone and to his surprise and horror, it was a single by The Seekers, 'Morningtown Ride'. He nearly died of embarrassment, but he put on a brave face. Even worse, we all had to suffer it as it was played constantly for Pass the Parcel and any other reason that mum could think of. Grandma never realised and she had tried her best to get him something he would like. She liked the song, it was number two in the charts that Christmas, and therefore she was sure he would love it. I don't think she ever knew anything different.

I suppose that it is part of the growing experience, but bit by bit, the older generation of family and guests began to disappear. First, my grandad passed away and a few years later, grandma. Those present still seemed to enjoy the occasion, but there was a tinge of sadness. The innocence of being a child gradually ebbed away and we became more reticent to perform and eventually, as teenagers, took any opportunity to separate ourselves, or excuse ourselves as soon as possible. It seems obligatory that teenagers are embarrassed by their parents and nothing they did ever changed that, but it was only a few years later that we appreciated what they did for us. I don't know if it is the same for girls, but boys spend the rest of their lives trying to undo some of the things they said and did to their parents. Maybe it was to fill the void, but elderly neighbours or people my mother knew from church, St. Wilfred's at Harehills, were invited and everyone seemed to have a great time. Of course, it was only a few years later that I married and had our first boy. Christmas then became very important again for us and we carried on the tradition. Everyone came to our house and we enjoyed the same games, the same food, the same jokes and the same laughter. Over time, we moved from being the youngsters, with wide-eyed wonder, and became the parents and now the senior ones. If you are lucky, you will share Christmas with others you love and keep your tradition alive.

WOODHOUSE FEAST AND ROUNDHAY PARK FAIR.

As a child, I remember the excitement of going to the fair. When I was little it was the small permanent funfair at Roundhay where there was a Helter-Skelter, some swing boats and a small roundabout with boats and buses on for the very young. I remember the joy of climbing the little stairs to the top deck of the little bus and it was something that my own children enjoyed when they were young. Not much changed over the years and, at first, Roundhay had a number of attractions. There was a maze, but this was removed in the 1970s, due to an incident that occurred there, rowing boats on the big lake and a small launch that took large numbers of people around the lake. I believe Roundhay School had a couple of boats on the big lake, which were used by the naval cadets. There was the Lakeside Cafe and kiosk which was a large wooden shed. There was also the Lido, an open air swimming pool near the back of Waterloo Lake. I went once or twice and even on the hottest days it was freezing cold. It also was removed, which is a shame, but probably the cost of the upkeep was prohibitive as there were so few days in a year when it could be used. There wasn't a cafe above the boatshed in these times, but when the Lakeside Cafe was demolished they built the cafe above the boatshed.

When I was young, the little fair was quite satisfying, but later we would go to Woodhouse Feast, near Leeds University, on Woodhouse Moor. These names obviously hark back to olden times where celebrations and feasting would take place to mark holy days and the like. The moor was close to the outskirts of Leeds City and was a suitable place for traders and tinkers to sell their wares, entertainers to ply their trade and for the locals to celebrate and have some fun. It also provided an opportunity for the young to meet and court, and for locals to purchase items not available at other times of the year. When I attended the feast, it had developed quite a lot, but still it was an opportunity to have fun, meet other young people, show off and spend money. As a child, we loved the lights, the sounds, the crowds and the smell that a fair brought. The workers appeared exotic, as they had a darker skin than most Leeds folk, used copious amounts of hair cream, wore tight black jeans and had tattoos. They called to passersby to get them to buy their wares or to try their hand to win a teddy, or in those days, plaster of Paris ornaments. There were roundabouts, Waltzers, swing boats, dodgems and a host of contraptions that would scare the living daylights out of you as a young child, but for teenagers, they were an opportunity to demonstrate your masculinity by fearlessly hanging off the bars as you were spun around, or by bashing your dodgem head on into another and laughing at the joy of it. The girls would been enraptured by the bravado of the fairground boys who danced between the whirling horses, collecting fees, darted between the dodgems, and hung off the bars at the back and walked backwards, collecting money on the waltzers as the floor went up and down. They never missed a beat, they were poised, relaxed, masters of impressing teenage girls. There were local lads who would emulate their feats, but due to lack of practice, they never quite cut the mustard.

For us kids, it was hook the duck, darts into playing cards, air rifle ranges, bran tubs, coconut shies and ping pong balls into goldfish bowls. The most sought after prize was a goldfish. The poor creatures were hanging in plastic bags and if you were lucky enough to win one, you would carry it around as a prized possession until you got home. My parents took us to the pet shop at Harehills, where we would buy a bowl, a little weed and goldfish food. With two brothers, there was a good chance that we would get at least one or two on a visit to a fair. In most cases, the poor fish would be lucky to live out the weekend, but the good news was that we were prepared for future fairs, with the bowl and equipment already waiting. In fairness, there were one or two fish that were clearly made of sterner stuff than the usual goldfish and they survived for much longer periods. I can remember well being entranced by their shimmering scales and their fluid movement around their restricted new homes.

It was not just the rides and prizes, the whole experience was a whirl of lights, sounds and smells. The ground underfoot was trodden into mud and you had to carefully step over electrical cables that ran from generators that thumped a rhythm in the background, almost drowned out by the blaring music of the time. Buddy Holly and the Crickets, Bill Hayley, Elvis and the like filled the air and added to the excitement. The fair was the facade of celebration, but lurking behind were the caravans and homes of the workers. Some were chrome, brightly painted and affluent, but most were fairly run-down. Lorries, trucks and vans were waiting to carry them to a new location after only a few days.

The senses were overloaded and smells of food wafted everywhere, tempting us to buy and taste their wares. Toffee apples, brandy snaps, doughnuts, ice creams, all were available as well as the truly magical candyfloss. The machines that spun the sugar were entertainment on their own. Lurid dyes were added: bright pink, green, yellow. They were sticky, sweet and must have cost almost nothing to make, but managed to extract the few remaining coins we had. It was a tired, but happy family that would return to the car, nurse our fish or other prizes and drive home.

There was a similar fair that would annually arrive at Roundhay Park. This dwarfed the permanent amusements, but I am sure they didn't mind the extra trade the main fair brought. This fair would be set on the rise up from the big lake and the Lakeside Cafe. It could have been the same as the one from Woodhouse, but I don't think so. It had all the same sort of entertainments, and one I had forgotten was the strength-testing machines. There were two main types. The originals used a large wooden mallet that was swung and hit a post and the strength was recorded on a gauge. The strongest of blows would sound a bell. The second type, which I think came later, involved a punch ball. You thumped the ball as hard as you could and it recorded the power on a large dial. The strongest blows would similarly sound a bell. These were another alternative for men and boys to demonstrate their physical prowess in front of potential admirers.

I do remember one specific incident on the dodgems when I was a teenager in the late 1960s. A group of us were there and it was an afternoon session that wasn't particularly busy. There was a group from Allerton Grange on some of the others and I was on one, as was my friend. Only about half the cars were running and there was the usual lad in the kiosk, controlling the power and another who was collecting money and policing behaviour. Times had changed a little and front-on collisions were supposedly banned. (Health and safety gone mad) This clearly hadn't been taken on board by the assembled teenagers and there were a lot of crashes, cheers, cries and general mirth. At the back of the car was a rod that went vertically to the wire netting that supplied the power to the car. At the top of the rod was a metal shoe that dragged along the netting, keeping the contact and the power supplied. I suppose this was the one part that wore out frequently and I think they just slotted onto the pole. On this occasion, there was a lad in one of the cars. There was a shouting and crashes, almost drowned out by music, but then I saw, almost in slow motion, two dodgems collide with great force. The rear end of one lifted and then crashed back down. It must have been a freak occurrence, but the metal shoe jumped off the top of the pole and fell onto the boy driving. The side of the shoe struck him on the forehead, just above the eye and then blood poured out and his face turned red. It all happened in a fraction of a second. The man in the kiosk must have seen what happened. The power was turned off and the cars just stopped. Everyone's attention was drawn to the poor lad. The man from the kiosk ran over, carrying what looked like a tea towel and he clamped it onto the forehead of the now sobbing lad. Nowadays, I am sure there would have been first aid kits and first aiders, but then there didn't appear to be. He was helped out of the dodgem and led away. I suppose an ambulance must have been called, but I didn't see it, and within seconds the dodgem was pushed to the side, power was restored and the show was back on. My friend and I saw him several weeks later and he was proud to show us his impressive scar. He was very lucky not to have lost his eye and I have no idea whether any inquiry into the accident happened, but maybe not. Parents were not as quick to sue as they are nowadays and accidents were more accepted without anyone needing to be blamed.

During the day, the fairs were reasonably safe and respectable places, and this was the case in the early evening, when children were still about. Later at night, however, I believe fights often broke out between local groups of boys and the fair workers. This may have been the result of jealousy, as the workers chatted up local girls. I never really saw this, but there was a reputation that the fair lads had knives and would use them. As the fifties and sixties moved through, there were also confrontations between teddy boys, mods, rockers and later skin heads. Adrenaline, testosterone and teenagers are a dangerous mix and I am sure that it has always been thus.

The fairs were always short-lived. There was a day or two of setting up and after five or so days, the fair was dismantled and they disappeared for a new venue, to return in another year. When they had gone, the ground was left trampled and weary, but in a surprisingly short time it recovered and there was not a trace, except for the memories of those who had attended.

BEING A BOY!

Having two brothers and no sisters limits my memories of growing up in Leeds in the 1950s-60s and so I apologise for the one-sided view. However, we did play with girls at times, so it is not all boys only. I am sure we had left Lawrence Avenue for Gipton Wood Crescent before I started Harehills, so these memories are up to the age of six.

I remember quite clearly playing out in the street with my elder brother and wandering around the local streets. I believe there was the wreck of an old scout hall behind where our house was and I have a memory of jumping and snapping sections of broken asbestos. There was also a 'slag heap' along Lawrence Road, and the remains of the pit tower that would have lowered the miners underground, but I assume they are all long-gone. We used to climb up the steep black slopes and look over the tops of the houses in the area. I think it was fenced, but there were gaps where the fence had been cut or trampled down.

There was also a beck that ran behind the houses across from our house on Lawrence Avenue and we used to spend many hours building dams and generally getting muddy and wet. It was a little wild strip and we had lots of fun. Some of the houses in the street were beautifully kept with greenhouses and beds full of flowers around manicured lawns, but ours was our playground and had a rockery and row of trees across the back. I remember once, my parents inheriting an old grandfather clock and as they wanted things modern, not old, we were allowed to play with it. It was laid flat in the garden and we used to sit on it, as it would become a canoe or raft in some adventure we were having. In retrospect, it was a real shame, but generally people wanted things that were modern. I remember games on TV to have competitions where there was a race with two teams and they had to smash a piano up into pieces and the first team to pass all the pieces through a foot-square hole were the winners. I think it was the start of the 'It's a Knockout' type game show. I remember the house we moved to in Gipton Wood Crescent having colourful leaded windows and my father spent days removing them and having plate glass fitted. The lead was removed and sold to scrap merchants, but the glass just thrown away. Such a shame, but the windows did make the house dark and the new ones made it much brighter and more modern. Nowadays, they would not suffer the same fate and people would treasure them, but times now are very different.

My father left, Uncle Jim Cameron and Grandma Cameron.

It was at about this time that I remember the first Hula Hoops appearing. We must have had access to one, as I remember giving it a go, but failing miserably. My love was comics: Dandy, Beano, Topper and Beezer, I believe. They were fascinating reading. Who couldn't be captivated by Lord Snooty and his pals, Dennis the Menace, The Bash Street Kids and the others? The best editions were ones with free gifts and amongst these was the Clapper. It was a folded piece of cardboard with a brown paper insert. If you held it by the corner and flicked it in a downwards motion, the brown paper section shot out causing a loud bang. We loved them, but I'm not so sure about the neighbours. Another freebie was the Twirler. This was two circles of card and you threaded string through the holes and you twirled the cards around, whilst holding each end of the string. When it was wound sufficiently, you pulled on both ends in a concertina motion and the card circles whizzed around, making a loud humming noise. Great fun! One of the comics had a 'did you know' section and it would have interesting facts from history and science, and I remember cutting out these sections and pasting them into a scrap book. I can still remember the tallest spire in Britain, and that Hans Holbein painted a portrait of Sir Thomas Moore and many other useful pieces of information. Well, useful if you are a boy.

Another craze that came in at various times during my childhood, were Clackers. These were two plastic balls on string and by holding the string in the middle and moving your hand up and down, the balls would bounce off each other and become a blur and produce a loud clacking noise. These became such big news that there were reports of wrist injuries. A second craze was Alien Antennae. These were sparkly balls on springs that fitted on a hairband and children and some adults, would walk about wearing them with pride. Probably the most famous craze was the Yo-yo. These became popular on many occasions and if you could master the skill of 'Walking the Dog' and other tricks, then you became a legend. Unfortunately, despite several yo-yos and hours of practice, I was only able to achieve the very basic up and down, and then for only a short time. Just another one of my failures in life!

Another joy at this very young age was the collecting of PG Tips cards. Each packet of tea would have a card and these included British butterflies, explorers, wild flowers, wildlife and many others. I think they were a child version of the cigarette cards and I loved to collect them. You could send off for the albums to stick them in and these were full of additional information. I did manage to get a full set of British Butterflies, but I think that was my only one. There must be something genetic about collecting things. Some people have it and others don't. Two of my four sons have definitely inherited it. I did start collecting stamps when I was at Harehills C.P. School and I remember buying packets of stamps from Ashton's sweetshop across the road from the school. There was great anticipation and delight in opening the packets and gazing at stamps from exotic-sounding countries that I had never heard of, and some with brilliantly-coloured illustrations. I still have some of the stamps and albums

from these days, stashed away. I had a theory and still think it is true, that the least desirable countries often have the most enticing stamps. My uncle went to Russia with work in the early 1960s and he brought back Russian stamps that showed their cosmonauts and even their first dog in space. I did save up my pocket money to buy the Stanley Gibbons' Stamp Catalogue in 1967.

Breakfast brought excitement sometimes, with the cut-out animal heads on the back of Cornflake packets. I was only allowed to have them when the packet was empty. I loved breakfast cereals: Cornflakes, Rice Crispies and Honey Smacks, with the cream off the top of the milk. I still don't think there is anything nicer, but now it is all low fat, low sugar, due to misspent youth. The animal heads: tigers, zebras, elephants, hippos and lions, were two dimensional models, that when cut out, tabs folded and glued in place, produced a three dimensional head. It wasn't the end product that I liked, but the process. Some were abject failures, but like most things, you get better with practice. I did once buy a book from Varley's that was a much more complicated kit of cardboard templates that made a pirate galleon. I spent ages making it, was frustrated by my lack of skill at scoring along the folds with a scissor blade and glueing, but in the end produced a reasonable model. Blue Peter had a lot to answer for! They made everything look so easy. 'Here is one I started earlier!'

Before the age of seven, my greatest pleasure was my toy soldiers. I had a wooden castle and I fought many battles between the knights. Varley's Toyshop at Harehills also used to sell little boxes of Airfix soldiers. These soldiers were tiny, but you got lots of them and there were so many kits. You had to separate every figure off the plastic frame and they ranged from World War II soldiers, to knights in armour, foreign legion, cowboys and red-indians. There were many on offer and they allowed the young mind to live out adventures. You could take them outside and hide them amongst the rockery and plants and fight out any battle you wanted. Trenches could be dug, mines and tunnels built with supporting beams of twigs or little forts with twig stockades. There really was no limit.

I am not sure that it is any different for children nowadays. Yes, they are provided with so much more, but really they disappear into their own world if given half a chance. Technology is a good child-minder, but not necessarily a great mind stimulator. Playing outside, whenever possible, was the first option, but this has sadly been taken away.

A BIT LATE

I realise that it is a little late to introduce my family, but if you have read this far, then you probably have got to know us pretty well. I can honestly say that I loved my childhood and loved my family. As a father and grandparent, I realise that if you can make your family's memories good ones, then you have achieved a lot. I hope that as you have read this, then your own experiences will have come to mind, bubbled to the surface and brought you pleasure. Not all can be lucky to have an ordinary childhood, but even the most ordinary are filled with incidents of drama, disappointment, challenge, failure, sadness, laughter and joy.

I started my Cup of Tea Tales blog, several years ago and it proved popular with those who shared many of my experiences, those who have an interest in the social history of the 1950s and 60s, and those who like short, interesting reads. I was asked to compile some of my many tales into a book and here it is. I hope that you enjoyed it and I will hopefully produce others in the future.

I have added a photograph of my parent's wedding in 1950. You may notice that my father has a sock over his left foot, as he had a steel-casting fall on it and crushed it just before the big day. He needed crutches and his foot was in plaster. Maybe this was just a sign of the adventures to come!

Mum and Dad's Wedding 1950.

ABOUT THE AUTHOR

David M Cameron was born in Leeds, in Yorkshire. He is married with four sons and two grandchildren. David has lived in England, Papua New Guinea and Perth Western Australia, where he has been for the last twenty-eight years. He has written two novels for children, Wickergate and Soulmare and the five books of The Moondial Series for adults. David also has a weekly blog of his 'Cup of Tea Tales' that tell some of his life's stories on growing up in Leeds during the 1950s.
More information on both David's music and books can be found on his website/blog:

http://davidmcameronauthormusician.com

Printed in Great Britain
by Amazon